If you have ever wondered, as I have, if you are making emotional and spiritual progress or your life is simply imploding, this is the book for you! For those seeking a new spiritual center this book will allow you to explore a range of options. If you are at a point of genuine desperation, "reinvention" may be the cool, refreshing, life-giving water for your dry, parched inner life, and a place of rest and replenishment for your weary soul.

Paul A. Brez, Colorado Suicide Prevention Commission

In an age of rapid change and fear, Michelle and Fe gift us with a model to navigate stormy waters. Based on extensive experiences culled from real-life stories, they chart a course that is wise, life giving, and inspiring. I heartily commend Life, Death, and Reinvention *as a spiritually and psychologically sound guide for all in transition.*

David B. Reynolds, Pastoral Counselor

The clarity of thought in Life, Death, and Reinvention *offers a roadmap to those who never believed they could begin again. In this book the authors do not leave their readers at the threshold of this journey but walk with them through the narrow door, guiding them in the wilderness and showing them the path to a reinvented life. Michelle and Fe Anam do so with great personal courage, gentleness, and wisdom.*

Rebecca L. McClain, Episcopal Clergy

This book is invaluable reading for all who stand on the precipice of reinvention and all who journey with them. Michelle Snyder and Fe Anam Avis offer a roadmap through the exciting and sometimes treacherous process of significant personal change that is rooted in compassion and deep spirituality. As one who has gone through the process of reinvention, I recognized myself in these pages, and as a therapist I found information that is useful and important for my clients.

Bryan Bass-Riley, CPE Supervisor and Training Director

LIFE, DEATH, AND REINVENTION

MAGI Press

LIFE, DEATH, AND REINVENTION

The Gift of the Impossibly Messed-Up Life

MICHELLE SNYDER
FE ANAM AVIS

LIFE, DEATH, AND REINVENTION
The Gift of the Impossibly Messed-Up Life

PUBLISHING CONSULTANT: Huff Publishing Associate, LLC
COVER IMAGE © Agsandrew | Dreamstime.com
COVER AND INTERIOR DESIGN: Marti Naughton

Published by MAGI Press.
ISBN: 978-0-9977687-1-8

MICHELLE'S DEDICATION

to Rob Guy

Your willingness to
journey with me through the desert
was manna from heaven.

☉☉

FE'S DEDICATION

to Richard and Kay Baumann

Who sheltered and befriended me
during my reinvention

TABLE OF CONTENTS

INTRODUCTION

This is a book about reinventing your life.

We begin with a definition. *Reinvention*: to significantly alter your patterns of living in a way that will expand your zest for life and capacity to contribute to the world.

It is important to clearly say that this book specifically addresses those who are in the midst of this reinvention process whether they are yet aware of it or not. With the possible exception of celebrities trying to expand market share, people generally do not choose to reinvent their lives on a whim. The process of reinvention is simultaneously exhilarating and excruciating, and the journey is often a lonely one. If you are a *reinventor,* this book is our best and most sincere attempt to be your companion and to invite you to join the growing band of others traversing this strange and wondrous terrain.

Other readers are welcome to this conversation, perhaps for the sake of the family members or friends of one who is reinventing, but we give you fair warning. You may find the urgings of this book unconventional and, in a few cases, even ill-advised. Grant us this concession—to maintain a life that is sound and satisfying differs significantly from what is required to entirely change a life that is drowning on a daily basis.

Imagine an aerial view of a community on a summer's day—neighbors conversing, children playing, someone mowing a lawn. Suddenly they all begin to pull ladders out of cellars and garages, climb to the roof, and sit there. Such behavior would appear inexplicable and unproductive, even dangerous. You certainly would advise against it.

Now simply add to your mental picture fifteen feet of floodwater in the street below. The addition of that single element radically changes how you view persons sitting on the roofs of houses.

Behaviors you previously judged strange or ill-advised now appear essential, even heroic in the face of a ravaging flood. How you evaluate the behavior of those in the scene will shift dramatically depending upon whether you see the threat of drowning. This is the perspective we use with people who need to reinvent their lives, except life is drowning them instead of water. Not everyone will be able to understand that perspective.

This is our first nugget of wisdom for reinventors: do not wait to reinvent your life until people around you understand. Many of them simply will not. Perhaps never. Here is why.

Samesiders and Othersiders

For the purposes of our conversation, there are two kinds of people in the world: *samesiders* and *othersiders*.[1] Samesiders are persons who have basically lived their entire lives in the same "neighborhood" of values, aspirations, relationships, and commitments. It's not that their lives haven't evolved in some significant ways, but any movement has been from one street to another, not to an entirely different part of the world. They may have left a Presbyterian church to join a Methodist church, but they didn't move from rural western Pennsylvania to join a Pentecostal mission serving food to the homeless on the streets of New York City. They may have left a lucrative, personal injury legal practice to do corporate law instead, but they didn't leave it all at age fifty-five to get a PhD in Mandarin and teach at a major university. They may have moved to a different part of the country that changed their address, but they likely didn't change their entire legal name. Many who might describe themselves as "born again" are also samesiders in that they are returning to the same faith in which they were raised, but with greater personal conviction.

It is a distinction better experienced than described, but there is a point at which a person crosses a threshold and realizes that he or she is not in Kansas anymore. When that line is crossed, an othersider is born. Othersiders are persons who have passed through a significant life experience that has required transformation as a condition of survival. In that process, the entire landscape has shifted.

As one variety of othersiders, people reinventing their lives are suddenly mysterious to their samesider families and friends. Samesiders often experience reinventors as foreigners who may as well be speaking in tongues. We have had to face this issue head on in writing this book. Trying to write a book that can be understood by both reinventors and samesiders is like trying to write a single book that can be understood by both Americans and Sentinelese.

As reinventors ourselves, we have written this book on the other side for those on the journey to becoming othersiders.

A Famous Reinventor

Some of the most notable people who have ever lived are persons who reinvented their lives. But people often aren't aware of their reinvention process because it preceded the significant achievements for which they are remembered. It might be fair to say that the most productive years for many people did not, indeed could not, occur until after their reinvention. Since samesiders outnumber reinventors, the reinvention part of the story is often ignored or forgotten.

See if you can guess the identity of a famous person we have renamed "Manny."

In his twenties, all signs were that Manny's life had headed south. He left his job, moved out of his home, and began to wander about the country. He got into trouble with the law. In a relatively short period of time he became homeless and lost all financial independence. He began living solely from the charity of others, particularly a group of married women who began to kick about with him. Manny's family, who had once adored him as a child, now alternated between thinking he was mentally ill to concluding that he was just a troubled person.

Manny's full name was *Immanuel,* but he wasn't Latino. He was the Jew, Jesus of Nazareth. It would surprise many people to learn that, with the exception of his name, all the information in the previous paragraph is factual. Looking simply at those facts, it would be easy to pathologize his life, but even those who cannot believe he was "God made man" would have trouble assessing his life as a failure. With the benefit of a longer time perspective, we realize that what we are observing in Jesus is not a life going south, but a life in the process of reinvention from that of carpenter to itinerate preacher and healer who would leave a major mark on history.

To you who are in the throes of reinvention where it feels like everything is falling apart, take heart. You are in very good company!

What Reinvention Looks Like

Here are five quick observations about reinvention.

- **Reinvention** is often messy and ambiguous. It is sometimes difficult to tell if a person is reinventing his or her life, or simply messing it up. Reinvention is not for the "most likely to succeed." Reinvention is the gift of the impossibly messed-up life.
- **Reinvention** is difficult for many members of a community, including family, to understand and support. Those relationships closest to a person during reinvention are sometimes the most difficult.
- **Reinvention** does not necessarily make people more holy (Jesus was already holy) or "better" people. By many measures Jesus was not a better person—they said he drank too much, ate too much, and kept company with prostitutes—but he was a different person with different capacities.
- **Reinvention** does not necessarily require a religious conversion. Jesus was born and died practicing his Jewish faith. There are many, many persons in faith communities who need to reinvent their lives, across all theological stripes.
- **Reinvention** is an essential, inescapable process for many persons if they are to make their full and unique contribution to the world.

The journey of Jesus is one template for reinvention, but it is not the only one. Reinventors come from a variety of faith traditions whose historical figures underwent their own reinvention: Buddha, Mohammed, Moses, Confucius, and Zoroaster to name a few. Some reinventors may not have a spiritual template. Given our particular faith tradition, we have found that the reinvention of Jesus offers helpful insights, even for those who may not accept the variety of doctrines that now surround him. The various aspects of reinvention can feel isolating and disorienting. Knowing that one of the most significant spiritual figures in history had a similar experience brings a sense of dignity to the process of reinvention, reassures us when we "feel crazy" or alone, and grounds us in a spiritual purpose.

What challenges do people likely encounter in the process of reinvention? Here we turn our attention to the period of time between Jesus' life as carpenter and his life as an itinerate preacher and healer.

The Bible has a considerable amount to say about this period. Apart from the account of his trial and crucifixion, the most detailed account of any experience of Jesus is the description of the time between his first life and his reinvented one. A portion of that time is called the "wilderness temptation."

The decision to reinvent his life plunges Jesus into a time of temptation. Putting the specific temptations aside for now, the severity of this experience is signified by the fact that 1) he is alone, 2) he is in the elements without shelter, and 3) the temptations are delivered to him by the most powerful "tempter" in the universe. The fact that it is the devil himself who poses these temptations indicates that we are not dealing with an amateur tempting us to eat a piece of chocolate. These are powerful, soul-shaking, brass-knuckled encounters. The process of reinvention is difficult, sometimes laced with anxiety about our own material security, and often requiring some of the toughest work we will ever do in resisting the internal voices that lead to abandonment of the process or even self-destruction.

For those who hear these words as discouragement, the exact opposite is the intent. All these experiences are normal, temporary, and, in retrospect, purposeful. Jesus' story provides the spiritual reassurance that you are not crazy, doomed, or off course.

While we can benefit greatly from studying the reinvention of Jesus and other historic figures, much of what we have learned about reinvention has been from real living persons.

Marty is a seventy-eight-year-old woman who exudes confidence and carries herself with a bearing characteristic of those with wealth and prominence. She is one of the wealthier women in North America. Her desire to live up to that image and her perfectionistic attention to detail made her parties and dinner gatherings the envy of her peers. Though her husband held the senior position at one of the top ten investment banking firms in the country, she had her own wealth that she had inherited and then leveraged through a chain of women's clothing stores.

In her late fifties Marty began to struggle with bouts of anxiety and depression. Her unhappiness puzzled her because she couldn't come up with a real reason for her depressed state. Her husband attributed it to a need for rest and scheduled more and longer vacations. These offered temporary relief, but upon her return to the demanding schedule, her deteriorating mood awaited her at the office door.

In order to maintain the appearance of a person who had it together, Marty felt she needed to pretend that everything was fine. But by her early sixties the high pressure and unrelenting pace began taking a toll on her physically. Eventually she was hospitalized with a mild stroke and uncontrolled hypertension. Her longtime physician made no bones about her condition: "Either change your life or you will die."

His admonition hit Marty like a punch to the gut. "I went home, cancelled my schedule, and sat for a month," Marty reflects. "I learned about a five-day workshop on meditation and healing in a book I was reading. By the end of that same day, I was signed up."

Marty had never been much of a religious person. She had grown up Jewish, but learned about the "Christ spirit," as she puts it, from her piano teacher. She didn't experience a conversion, but she did begin to take spirituality seriously. She attended multiple retreats and started practicing healing meditation. Today a number of people trace their near miraculous recoveries to Marty's spiritual practices.

Many of Marty's friends became uncomfortable with this stranger that talked to them about angels and guides and the "Christ spirit." Family members also started keeping distance. Initially, her husband was confused as well, but he has grown to appreciate Marty's new life and the vitality it has restored to her.

At age sixty-three she turned over her business to others and now serves in an advisory role that only requires a few hours a month of her time. Her days are structured around reading, meeting with other spiritual companions, healing, and growing flowers. She gives large sums of money to charities, especially those helping the ill and infirm.

The Five Stages of Reinvention

In Marty's story, we see the five elements that characterize reinvention.

- **Contradiction**—sensing a fundamental inconsistency between the way life should be and the way life actually is, combined with a pretense that nothing has changed.
- **Collapse**—the pressure of the contradiction builds internally until it erupts into the physical world of time and space.
- **Clarity**—a growing level of self-awareness and acceptance of the amount of change required.
- **Commitment**—an intention is set with creative, yet concrete steps to bring life back into alignment with all the resultant gains and losses.
- **Coherence**—a reconstruction of life around new, more sustainable themes.

Contradiction. Marty is puzzled by the fact that all the assets in her life are not sufficient to produce happiness. She believes she should be happy but she experiences depression and anxiety instead. She is experiencing a contradiction between what she believes about life and the way life actually is, but pretending that nothing has changed.

Collapse. Since Marty is not ready to deal with the meaning of the contradiction, she lives with it. As a result, she keeps making decisions that serve to deepen the contradiction. More and longer vacations that should make her feel better only worsen her emotional state. Eventually her body falters under the pressure much like a blown fuse.

Clarity. In an extended period of reflection, Marty begins to face what is going on inside her. She becomes clear about a direction to move.

Commitment. Marty identifies a concrete step she can take in a genuinely new direction: going on a retreat. She takes steps even though they may result in some losses. She is bolstered in her commitment by the seriousness of what will happen if she returns to life as she has lived it. She is also finding that her steps forward are resulting in positive experiences. She is possessed by a clear sense that she is being guided or carried by a force greater than herself.

Coherence. Marty goes through a process of reconstructing her life around themes of spirituality, healing, and generosity. New opportunities consistent with those themes "coincidentally" appear.

We have seen this pattern in the lives of reinventors over and over again. It is not intended to be a formula. God does not give us blueprints. God does give us fingerprints that serve as evidence we are being guided or carried by something greater than ourselves. We have found that as reinventors enter this process, a spiritual conspiracy begins to assist them in their process from death to life.

Entering at Your Own Point in the Journey

This book is for persons reinventing their lives. As a reinventor, you may find yourself at any point in this process. You may be an attorney anticipating retirement who believes that life will be "just like now except without the stress." You may be realizing that the universe doesn't work that way. You're in contradiction.

You may be in the agony of full collapse, in the realignment of thinking required by the clarity stage or in the Edison-like, trial and error stage of commitment. You may be realigning all the elements of your life in the coherence stage. Don't hesitate to jump into the book matching where you are, but you will probably find it helpful to go back and see how you got there by reading earlier chapters!

Many persons have gone through the reinvention process but do not have the language to describe their journey. These reinventors will benefit from reading this book and being able to say, "Oh! That's what happened to me!"

Finally, if you know someone that you suspect is going through a reinvention process, give that person this book and offer to walk with him or her through the process. There is no greater gift you can give another. Parker Palmer writes of "the most profound form of leadership I can imagine—leading a suffering person back to life from a living death" (from *Let Your Life Speak: Listening for the Voice of Vocation*).

Part One of this book looks in more detail at this five-stage process of reinvention. Part Two examines the places that people tend to get stuck and offers some thoughts on how to get unstuck. Part Three explores some resources that reinventors like ourselves have found helpful.

Take a deep breath, summon your courage, and turn the page.

THE FIVE STAGES
OF REINVENTION

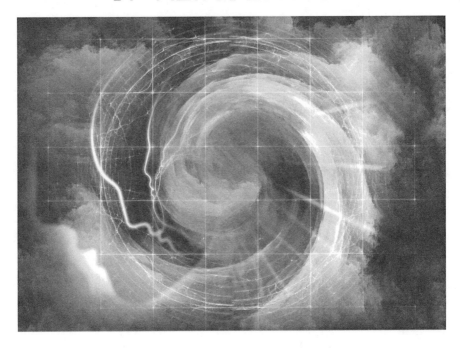

CONTRADICTION

Melissa grew up in a church where praying prayers of faith was central to life. She was taught to pray bold prayers predicated on the fact that people do not *have* because they do not *ask*. Ask and you shall receive. Seek and you will find. Knock and the door will be opened. To do less was to degrade one's status as a beloved child of God. Faith was all that mattered. Without faith one could not succeed.

With faith, all things were possible. Failure in prayer was a sign of inadequate faith or sin in one's life.

These beliefs actually served Melissa well for much of her life. She can tell a number of remarkable and convincing stories of answered prayers that characterize the lives of those with robust, spiritual practices. It all made for a comfortable existence until the period when two crises hit her in rapid succession: her grandfather was diagnosed with terminal cancer and her mother left her father for another man. As with every other crisis, she prayed her prayers of faith, but this time there was no apparent response. The formula that had previously enabled her to thrive no longer solved the problem. The universe was not working the way she thought it did. To make things worse, she could not share her changing views with her faith community for fear of rejection. She began to pretend.

This experience is not unique to Melissa. In one of the more interesting passages of the New Testament, Jesus and his disciples came upon a man who had been blind from birth. "Who sinned," they asked of Jesus, "this man or his parents?" (John 9:2, NIV). Their question started from an assumption that good deeds are rewarded and bad deeds are punished. This is called the "just universe" theory. The disciples believed that every human malady could be traced back to sins committed, either those of the individual or the individual's parents. In Jesus' response to their question, the disciples experienced a contradiction. They discovered that life does not work the way they thought it did. Their old paradigms for living were no longer a sufficient infrastructure to support their way of seeing the world.

What Contradiction Looks Like

Soul-shaking contradictions take many forms.

A time-honored adage says work hard and you will get ahead. Instead you then find that your PhD in English literature only earns you an adjunct position where you barely make minimum wage. A fraudulent investor draws you into a Ponzi scheme where your life savings is lost. You build a law practice that is virtually unparalleled only to find that it has cost you your relationships with your children.

People might believe at their core that God helps those who help themselves. But then, in spite of a lifelong healthy diet and daily exercise, someone has a premature and debilitating stroke. A person works eighty hours a week to make ends meet but an underfunctioning neighbor wins the lottery. A mother sacrifices much to raise her daughter with morals and values only to find her daughter addicted to pain meds and engaged in criminal behavior to support her habit.

For some, once these cracks have started to form, there can be a domino effect. We call it the "great unraveling."

As with both Melissa, mentioned earlier, and the disciples, what happens in contradiction is the beginning of an inversion of one's values. As the belief structure on which one's life is built starts to crumble, one scrambles for new places to call home. As old assumptions prove faulty, ideas once refused now are considered and find their way into one's thinking. As old relationships turn out to not be what one thought, people once cast aside are given a second look.

What one once believed was important no longer is, or what one had no time for before, now becomes a priority. What was once deemed sinful or heretical is now the very pathway to experience God in a new and life-giving way.

Samesiders and Reinventors

One of the fundamental differences between samesiders and reinventors is that samesiders are able to avoid contradiction by taking in new information in a way that makes it fit their current view of life. Jean Piaget, a developmental psychologist, called this *assimilation*. Assimilation, Piaget observed, occurs when external information is taken in and processed through existing categories. Ideas about the world are reinforced when new information is consistent with one's beliefs regarding how the world works. Often the new information is even squeezed into one's current schemata, at the expense of occasionally distorting it.

In the children's book *Fish Is Fish* by Leo Lionni, a fish and a tadpole live together in a pond and are friends. One day the tadpole becomes a frog and leaves the pond. When he returns to visit his friend the fish, he tells the fish all that he has seen, such as cows and birds and people. But because the fish has only one schema for life, he pictures the cows as fish with legs and the birds as fish with wings. This is assimilation. The samesider fish avoided contradiction by having only one cubbyhole into which he or she made everything fit.

Here is an example of someone named Randy. Randy felt socially inept and not very likeable most of his life. It wasn't until his mid-thirties that he made a friend, Barry, who found him highly interesting. For Randy to accept the information that he was actually likeable might introduce a contradiction into his life. He could avoid that contradiction and remain a samesider by assimilating that information into his existing understanding of himself, denying that Barry knew what he was talking about. He could find ways to explain away Barry's interest and opinion by saying there must be something wrong with Barry. Deciding that Barry had a hidden agenda for his comments and that he couldn't possibly really mean them exemplifies a natural way of assimilating new information into an old paradigm.

In contrast, reinventors have reached a point in their life where they can no longer do that. Piaget named this *accommodation*. Accommodation, Piaget says, occurs when people are confronted by information that simply does not fit inside the cubbyholes, or schemata, of their minds, hearts, and psyche. When this happens, they are often forced to tear down old cubbyholes and build new ones. In the case of Randy, if he were to accommodate the experience of Barry's interest in him, he would need to reconsider the idea that he was socially inept and would be forced to open up to the possibility that he is more interesting than he once thought. He would consider the possibility that Barry saw something in him that was there, which Randy had been missing all along.

Both assimilation and accommodation are relatively common phenomena that happen to everyone all the time. But sometimes accommodation becomes more significant. An accommodation doesn't deepen into a contradiction until a person feels that he or she must pretend that it is not happening for fear of social consequences.

In the movie *Pleasantville,* a 1950-esque community lives its entire collective life in black and white. Slowly, some characters are exposed to spectacular beauty, sexuality, sensuality, and all other manner of emotional intensity that brings about personal transformation in them. As a result of these experiences, the once black-and-white characters start turning into color. Since the black-and-white community finds all this new color very threatening to the status quo, some members decide to put on makeup to hide their "color." It's a good movie on its own, but it's also an excellent cinematic example that illustrates contradiction.

Some contradictions (like those mentioned above) are triggered by the failure of life (or God) to live up to one's expectations of how life should be. Contradictions also can be encountered when an experience introduces the possibility that life is more than what one thought it ever *could* be. People experience contradiction when shaken from the status quo of a black-and-white life. They encounter something that they come to find life giving and life sustaining that, in one form or another, is deemed socially or morally unacceptable. To use the parable of Pleasantville, once people have "seen color" (sometimes for the very first time), they can no longer pretend they haven't.

But to admit they've seen color would be socially ostracizing. Seeing color can take many forms: a redefining near-death experience, a soul-stirring romance that was unanticipated but nevertheless undeniable, or a spiritual awakening that opens their eyes to whole new vistas of colorful truth.

Finding vigor and zest in what the rest of the world would call "strange," "ill-advised," or even "ungodly" (remember what they said about Jesus!), is often a place of significant contradiction. Contradiction is coming to the conclusion that life no longer works the way one thought it did combined with the need to pretend. Contradiction, then, can be quite painful because to reconcile the contradiction would require socially deconstructing some of the basic foundations upon which one's entire life has been built. That's when pretending begins.

Contradiction = (the way you thought life worked) – (the way life really works) + (pretending).

While there may be many reasons why accommodation turns into the pretending of contradiction, this often happens in two basic places. The first is when one has so much invested in the status quo that to accommodate the new information would have significant impact on the people, places, and things in one's life. Consider Cathy, the pastor who is coming to the conclusion that she can no longer believe in the God about whom she has been preaching. Her vocation, her livelihood, and her peer relationships will be significantly impacted if she accommodates her new ideas of God, but neither can she any longer preach with integrity what her congregation has come to expect from her.

Or consider Bill, a Methodist pastor who came to faith from atheism but was in a marriage to a woman who scorned his newfound faith. He said, "As my faith was increasingly life-giving, the gulf between that and the destructive forces of the life I had built was becoming increasingly wide. Unfortunately, those destructive forces included my marriage and my profession."

In one case, someone was moving away from the God she had known. In the other case, someone was moving towards a God he had never known. But for both people, the experience was one of contradiction.

Reinvention and Mental Illness

In Michelle's clinical practice, she often finds this internal contradiction manifests in a number of ways that can look like mental illness. Let us be clear: we strongly believe that mental illnesses are legitimate medical diagnoses. But it is equally true to say that when contradiction reaches a certain threshold, it can manifest as depression, anxiety, self-medication, or any number of other "adjustment disorders." There is no easy way through contradiction. The layers of one's life have been constructed in such a way that all the low-hanging fruit has been picked.

The easiest ways of improving a zest for living have already been taken—the added hobby or exercising or a yoga class.

Then one finds oneself like Alice in Wonderland, in a great hall surrounded by doors but all the doors are locked. When a person finds himself or herself in this situation, one will often become "depressed." It is our contention that the mental health community has erred on the side of helping people medicate away their contradiction instead of actively journeying with them through the challenges of reinvention.

In addition to the contradictions that develop from an investment in the status quo, contradictions also develop when the systems in which people live resist accommodation. Sometimes it is less that they are afraid to change their thinking and belief structure, but that they find themselves in systems that are actively working to keep them from doing so.

In the earlier example about Melissa, when she tried to discuss her experience of disconnect between what she had always been taught about God and what she was experiencing in the world, a leader in her Christian organization told her to "stop spreading her poison to the children." Often families and faith communities are ill prepared to deal with the "new" person that would be created if one were going to accept a new worldview. Systems will resist change because any one person in the system who changes throws the whole system into disorientation until it can find its footing again. Often that systemic resistance only intensifies the contradiction a person feels within.

The Signs of Contradiction

How do you know if you are in contradiction? Here are some signals that often characterize contradiction. Of course, no one of these in isolation is an indication of contradiction alone. But if multiple things on this list give you pause, you may be in a state of contradiction. You may be feeling:

- **Isolated and lonely**—You believe that few people in your life would understand what you were thinking and feeling if you told them. You find yourself attempting to explain "how you are" less and less often. You keep to yourself internally while pretending to have it together on the outside.
- **Trapped**—Given all those who are depending on you "staying the same" you see no way out of the present situations in which you find yourself.

- **Alienated**—You realize that if you were to be honest about what you are doing, who you are becoming, or what you are thinking, you would be ostracized from your community and the people in your life. For this reason, you feel ostracized already.
- **Inauthentic**—The only way you have found to continue on with your current life is to pretend you think things you no longer do, pretend you aren't doing things you are, and pretend you are doing things you aren't.

You may be having thoughts like:
- "Am I losing my mind?"
- "Am I the only one who thinks this way?"
- "Am I the only one who sees the world like this?"
- "The only thing more intolerable than leaving is staying. And the only thing more unimaginable than staying is leaving."
- "If I tell people what I'm thinking, they will reject me, laugh at me, or try to change my mind."

You may be having physical symptoms:
- Chest pains
- Digestive issues
- Hypertension
- Panic attacks
- Exhaustion
- Insomnia
- Tension headaches

Try as they might, most people are unable to live very long in a state of contradiction. When two tectonic plates within the earth collide, tension will build internally for a time. At the surface nothing appears to be changing. Eventually the inevitable earthquake will shake the foundations of everything that has been built.

Steps to Take in the Contradiction Stage

If you are in a state of contradiction, we suggest the following steps.

1. Now may be the time to find a therapist familiar with reinvention. If you can't find one, offer a solid therapist this book and invite him or her on the reinvention journey with you. In other words, do not try to do this alone.

2. Trust that others have been where you are and come out on the other side with a zest for living. Trust that you are not alone even if you can't identify right now who the people are in your life you can trust with contradictions. Trust that you are not losing your mind. Trust that we are with you in this.

3. Commit to tell someone if you begin to think about suicide. Some people in a state of contradiction begin to see suicide as their only option. Make a list of three people you will tell if you ever start to feel that way. (See Chapter Nine "Dealing with Suicidal Thinking.")

4. Settle in for the journey. Reinvention doesn't happen fast. You didn't get here overnight and you're not going to get out of it overnight. Give your mind periods of rest. Contradiction tends to exhaust us by burning a lot of internal mental processing. Let us give you a roadmap forward.

The good news is that if you begin reinventing at the contradiction stage, you can often navigate the rest of the process more intentionally—and less painfully.

For many reinventors, the contradiction stage does not provide sufficient motivation to begin that process. Then they find that motivation in the next stage: collapse.

2

COLLAPSE

The I-35W Mississippi River bridge was an eight-lane, steel truss arch bridge that carried traffic across the Saint Anthony Falls of the Mississippi River in Minneapolis, Minnesota. The bridge was Minnesota's fifth busiest, carrying 140,000 vehicles daily. On Wednesday, August 1, 2007, with rush hour bridge traffic moving slowly through the limited number of lanes, the central span of the bridge suddenly gave way, followed by the adjoining spans. The structure and deck collapsed into the river and onto the riverbanks below, the south part toppling eighty-one feet eastward in the process. The collapse killed 13 people and injured 145.

The collapse of a major bridge bearing almost a quarter of a million persons across the Mississippi River every day was a shock to most Americans who travel across such bridges without a second thought.

To a small number of inspectors, however, the collapse was not much of a surprise at all. Here is the record.[1]

- In 1990 inspectors gave the bridge a rating of "structurally deficient," citing significant corrosion in its bearings.

- According to a 2001 study by the civil engineering department of the University of Minnesota, cracking had been previously discovered in the cross girders at the end of the approach spans. Resistance to motion at the connection point bearings was leading to out-of-plane distortion and subsequent stress cracking.

- In 2005 the bridge was again rated as "structurally deficient" and in possible need of replacement.
- In a separate study in 2005, the bridge was given a safety rating of 50 out of a possible 100 points. Only 4 percent of the heavily used bridges in the county had a worse rating.
- The inspection carried out June 15, 2006, found problems of cracking and fatigue.
- At the time of the collapse, four of the eight lanes were closed for resurfacing, and there were 575,000 pounds of construction supplies and equipment on the bridge.

So when did the collapse of the I-35 bridge begin? It began in 1990 with the corrosion of its bearings invisible to everyone except those inspectors who knew how to go inside it. It didn't become visible to most people until sixteen years later when rivets started snapping on August 1, 2007, at 6:05 p.m.

"For who knows a person's thoughts except their own spirit within them?" (1 Cor. 2:11, NIV). The only person who lives inside of you is you. You are the sole "inspector" who experiences the cracking and fatigue of your inner structures. Contradiction may work invisibly for years to break down a soul, but the first thing others usually see is the collapse.

What Collapse Looks Like

There are many different ways lives collapse. In an adaption of a principle developed by Anna Karenina: "Happy individuals tend to be all alike; collapsing individuals tend to collapse in their own way." One way to think of this is to look at the six emotions that are hardwired into the human brain. Only one of these—happiness— releases positive hormones into the bloodstream. The other five—fear, anger, disgust, sadness, and surprise—release stress hormones that can compromise physical and emotional health, damage relationships, and impede one's ability to achieve meaningful goals. There are 120 different combinations of these negative emotions that can prove harmful if they become pervasive and persistent.

Perhaps that is why there are so many different ways that people describe the experience of collapsing: I am falling apart . . . I am having a breakdown . . . I am having a meltdown . . . I am losing it . . . I am going crazy . . . I am going to the dogs . . . I am going to hell in a handbasket . . . I am going nuts . . . I am going off the deep end . . . I am wigging out . . . I am freaking out . . . I am going bananas . . . I am going mental . . . I am going postal . . . and I have hit rock bottom, just to name a few. (We will come back to one of our favorites—I am going to pot—in a few paragraphs.)

Notice that all these expressions describe a process of collapsing, something deteriorating rapidly. In contrast there is no corresponding list of phrases that describe the process of becoming happy. This is significant. It suggests that the pathways to bliss are few, while those leading to collapse are many. This is consistent with great spiritual teaching across the ages. "But small is the gate and narrow the road that leads to life" (Matt. 7:14, NIV).

Collapse involves more than a string of a few bad days. Collapse introduces a person to week after week of feeling painfully disoriented. Collapse is the result of multiple contributaries of contradiction flowing into the same river creating a riptide. Things one assumed were enduring begin to crumble, even vanish. A person loses confidence in one's ability to know what is real. One's mind scrambles from one handhold to another, but each gives way. Nothing seems sturdy enough to finally break a fall. It becomes difficult to trust one's perceptions.

People can usually solve problems in their life by focusing on them one at a time. In contrast, a collapsing life is usually deteriorating along a number of fronts at the same time. In fact the word *collapse* comes from two Latin words that mean "slip together." Often the different aspects of the collapse are connected. A person who is despairing about a job that is not a good fit can't leave it without creating financial pressure on a household, which impacts relationships, which impacts stress levels, which impacts health, which impacts ability to perform on the job, and so forth. Someone once described this feeling of collapsing as "trying to extinguish a forest fire with a garden house while it moves in all around me."

With time many situations can be reversed: relationships can be reconciled, debt can be eliminated, and health can be restored. But a collapsing life has significant losses that can never be recovered.

Death of a loved one is obviously irreversible. Despite the best efforts of both parties, a divorce can result in the permanent loss of friendships and family relationships. Church members who go through a divorce and find their faith community ostracizing and isolating are often amused to find that they are welcomed with open arms into a neighboring faith community just down the block. Yet the pain of lost relationships remains.

A collapsing life has no short-term solutions. If there were a quick fix, people would have applied it a long time ago. Given the right amount of flexibility, a change in the place one lives can happen quickly.

Rebuilding trust or changing the relationship with a toxic family system can take years or sometimes never occurs.

The prospect of collapses along multiple fronts combined with the pain of permanent losses that cannot be relieved quickly often leads to despair and even suicidal thinking, the ultimate collapse. About 6 percent of adults in the United States are considering suicide. For many friends and family members, a suicidal collapse of a loved one comes as a surprise even though cracks in the soul have been developing for years. While suicidal thinking is always to be taken very seriously, it can also be a great gift because it exposes the internal deterioration and pain a person has been trying to patch together and alleviate, sometimes for many years. Suicidal thinking can often be just the collapse that is needed for someone to reinvent his or her life.

The Gift of the Impossibly Messed-Up Life

Think back to the story of the I-35 bridge.

The bridge collapsed in 2007. The US Department of Transportation's National Bridge Inventory had recommended that the bridge be rebuilt in 2005. But in spite of that recommendation, Governor Tim Pawlenty indicated the bridge was not scheduled to be replaced until 2020, fourteen years after the disaster. It took the collapse to provide the motivation to rebuild the bridge that, incredibly, was accomplished in one short year. The collapse accelerated rebuilding.

We would be remiss if we did not acknowledge that collapse is occasionally catalyzed by one's own choices. Notice that we didn't say *created* by one's own choices. As we have said previously, collapse is a result of contradictions that generate numerous cracks over time. But occasionally, or maybe even often, within the chaos of the collapsing infrastructure of people's lives—out of their desperation and disorientation—people make choices that catapult their lives into full-blown collapse. Marital infidelity might be one example of just such a catalyst. In therapy, Michelle sees case after case of couples coming to counseling when their marriage has collapsed because of an affair. Nearly without exception, it becomes clear over time that the cracks of contradictions had been forming in their relationship for years, sometimes decades. It might be that a person succumbed to temptation in the midst of one's desperation. It also might be that a new relationship opened a person's eyes and heart in a way that was once closed off, even to oneself. Michelle often sees that the onset of an adulterous relationship that makes someone feel alive after many years of feeling flat and uninterested can be the catalyst that forces a person to admit that he or she can no longer live in a world of gray.

Addiction or money laundering or workaholism are just a few examples of ways that one's behaviors can precipitate a collapse. So is the enlightenment of a return to higher education, the freedom of getting a job after years of being a stay-at-home spouse, or meeting a soul mate who sparks a passion that one has never before known. A collapse that is catalyzed by one's own choices, whether they are regrettable choices or not, makes it easy to lose sight of the real point, which is that this collapse didn't happen overnight. In spite of possible shame felt by a single action, experience, or the inability to hold one's life together, one's life has likely needed to change for some time.

Unfortunately this is often not how collapse is viewed by the general, outside observer. If you find yourself in collapse, you will likely experience any number of the following responses.

- Invisibility, with acquaintances and family members pretending you're not there. People will pretend your collapse is not happening and interactions that would have once been meaningful become superficial.
- Some well-intentioned folks may try to "fix you."
- Some people may be hurtful, some puzzled, and some genuinely concerned.
- Anger may be expressed by those who had different expectations of you.
- Action may be threatened against you, both legal and professional.
- You may end up taking care of other people in their concern for you.
- You may feel like there is no bottom to the free fall.

- Your reputation may be slandered, publically or informally.
- You learn who your friends really are, and you are surprised by some of the realizations.

But here's the good news. However you got here, by choices you made or circumstances outside your control, as difficult as the experience of collapse is, it often does serve the useful function of accelerating the reinvention process. This is the gift of the impossibly messed-up life. After years of trying to pave over the contradictions in your life in an effort to maintain some semblance of normalcy, collapse brings that phase to a necessary end. It blocks the path of return to the status quo and offers the motivation that can fuel the reinvention process. In order for the constructive power of collapse to begin to reshape the mind, you need a different image from that of something falling apart.

Clearing Away the Underbrush

We mentioned the person in collapse who described it as trying to put out a forest fire with a garden hose. We find this image to be quite helpful. Ironically, sometimes letting a forest fire burn is precisely the ingredient necessary for collapse. We see this in a species of tree known as the Bishop pine. The seeds of a Bishop pine are tightly sealed in the tree's cones by a resin that binds the cones shut until melted by a forest fire. The fire that appears destructive actually serves to release new seeds while clearing the competitive underbrush around a Bishop pine, preparing the way for new life.

Collapse serves the same function in the human soul.

Such images are more than saccharine fantasy. The human brain is much more likely to generate negative images than positive ones. The multitude of phrases listed previously elicits mental images such as drowning, broken machinery, and living on garbage eaten by dogs. Over time, these images can reshape our brains and serve to make us more fearful and angry, more forgetful, and less able to think creatively. But as a pastor once said, "We believe the stories we tell ourselves. If you tell yourself a new story, you will begin to believe that too." Cognitive-behavioral theory would agree.

Here is one more image that might be helpful. It comes from the phrase "my life is going to pot." In the days of the industrial revolution and early mass production, assembly workers would occasionally find a defective or out-oftolerance part that was not suitable for use. This part would be sent back to the smelting room to be melted down and recast a second time. Since the smelting was done in a giant pot, these defective parts had "gone to pot."

When your life goes to pot it is going through a meltdown, all in preparation for re-creation, this time in a form that is much more suitable to who you are at this point in your life. This provides a mental image that is positive and supportive of reinvention.

Steps to Take in the Collapse Stage

If you are in collapse, here are some things we recommend.

1. Practice daily seeing yourself as a pinecone with seeds being liberated by the fire burning all around you. It is not enough to simply think this thought. You must take a few minutes each day to envision the pinecone in your mind. See the fire destroying everything around it. See the resin melting in the pinecone. See the seeds being released. See new life springing from the ground. See the new forest that would not be possible without the fire. Now imagine you are that pinecone.

2. Know that collapse is the most concentrated, painful part of this reinvention journey. Listen deeply to us saying that while it feels like there is no bottom to your free fall, there is. Your life will not always look this way.

3. Journaling may be helpful at this point. If you feel unable to express all your painful emotions externally, getting them out on paper can often help with symptom relief. Make lists of all you are losing. Write about your shame and humiliation. Write about your anxiety and your fear. Do not keep that inside but also be selective about who you tell. When in doubt, your journal is a safe and trustworthy friend.

4. Did you find that reinvention therapist? Are you seeing him or her? If not, do. If so, keep it up.

5. Did you make the list of people you would tell if you are ever thinking about suicide? Keep it close. Use it if you need it.

When you feel ready to read on, we invite you to journey into clarity.

3

CLARITY

It was just after 1:00 a.m. on a cold February night in Plano, Texas. Rex Benson awoke to the smell of smoke in his bedroom. He moved quickly to waken the other two persons living in his home including an adult daughter. All three escaped the swiftly moving fire. Then events took a tragic turn. Mr. Benson went back into the burning house to get his cell phone. He could not escape the fire a second time. Experienced fire fighters say that 90 percent of persons who reenter a burning building do not come out alive.

Just as there is a natural tendency for a person to run back into a burning building to salvage the remnants of a previous life, persons can get stuck in the collapse described in the last chapter and never experience reinvention. Sometimes this happens because they think they can limit the damage through some heroic effort at holding up a few remaining walls. Sometimes people stay in collapse because they think, given enough time, they can fix it and return their lives to a previous state.

The Two Doors: Reinvention or Restoration

A critical decision must be made: Am I going to reinvent my life or am I going to seek to restore my life to a previous state? (A reminder: this book is written primarily for the reinventor.) We know of many examples where people have restored their life to great outcome. Many people stand at this pivotal place and choose, for very good reason, the path of restoration. Restoration is sometimes the right choice, and this chapter, in part, is to help you discern deeply which path is right for you. We believe that if you chose the path of restoration, the world is full of resources. We are committed to creating a resource for the reinventor.

Here is a concrete image to consider. Imagine you are in that burning house that is collapsing. You look around to see that there are only two doors leading out. One of the doors is marked RESTORATION. The other is marked REINVENTION. Now you must discern which door you will walk through.

We have found it helpful to spend some time reflecting on the situation in this way. Your life has just collapsed in any one of a thousand ways. It is possible, maybe even likely, that you have done something to precipitate the collapse. It is also possible that you are becoming aware of your own brokenness that contributed to the collapse, such as a previous trauma in your life, a degree of clinical depression, an anxiety disorder, or an addiction issue. In any event you are disoriented and shell-shocked. For many there will be an impetus toward restoration. Think about the biblical story of the prodigal son who did the hard work of restoring his familiar and comfortable life through confession and repentance. That will work for some. But for others, life as you know it is over and taking the path of restoration is like running back into a burning building that is no longer structurally sound or sufficient.

Three Ways of Viewing Your Collapse

There are several frames through which you can view what has happened to you. Our language is direct but know that we speak with no judgment. We have both been there. In addition it is likely that we are not going to say anything here that you have not already considered.

Sin. You HAVE messed up. You have failed. You have made poor decisions. You have fallen to temptation. You have to take responsibility. You need forgiveness, repentance, and assurance, all in an atmosphere of grace.

The question becomes: "What must I do to be saved?"

Sickness. You ARE messed up. You are broken, damaged, traumatized, injured, burned-out, depressed, maladjusted, PTSD-ing. You have to recognize what has happened TO you. You need healing (also grace), respite, therapy, perhaps even medication, and so forth.

The question becomes: "What must I do to be healed?"

Signal. You ARE BEING MESSAGED. Life as you have known it has come to an end. Life is falling apart in anticipation of a new creative process. Maybe you HAVE messed up, but life needed to fall apart anyway. Maybe you ARE broken, but putting a "healed" you back into the old life will just break you again.

As one reinventing person said, "Many people are pleading with me to 'come home' but they don't mean the new me. What they mean is 'come back to who you were, what you believed, what you valued, and how you lived.'" For many reinventors, that is impossible.

The question becomes: "What will you give in exchange for your soul?"

It is likely that all three—sin, sickness, and signal—were present in your collapse in one form or another. But like instruments in a symphony, different instruments need to be brought in at different points and at different intensity to make the right song. Playing one instrument too loudly can wreck the whole score. The task of discernment is the work of putting each of these in their rightful place so that you can know whether to walk through the REINVENTION door or the RESTORATION door.

The Restoration Door

If the *primary* issues are "sin" and "sickness," then restoration may be the door you need to take. The clarity of recognizing that some things need to change may very well lead a person to work at restoring their old life from a new perspective, with new attitudes and behaviors. The work of restoration may involve growing in self-awareness, making amends, asking forgiveness, changing relational patterns, rebuilding trust, and returning to the old life by a new path.

The work of restoration may also uncover elements of brokenness that require healing as part of the restorative process. Clinicians are now highly trained to help individuals recognize how trauma from the past or genetic predispositions toward particular mental health conditions can negatively impact relationships, self-image, and the ability to achieve important goals.

If you choose the restoration door, this book is not for you. While a desire for restoration exists to some degree in every person (even in those who are clear about their need to walk through the door of reinvention), walking through the restoration door means that most of your time and energy will focus on salvaging and repairing a former way of life. There are many books to help people faithfully do that. It simply is not this one.

The Reinvention Door

On the other hand, if the *primary* issue is "signal," reinvention becomes your option. However you got here, you are headed to places unknown because there is no home to return to. Whatever shape the collapse has taken, you realize that you are no longer willing to sacrifice your own soul for the sake of what was. Even suicidal thinking can be an indication that something needs to die—it's just not you.

Reinvention may be the option for those who feel that they have been catapulted forward by a crisis. The reinvention door offers a face-forward orientation and a sense of personal dignity. While they can't know what the future might hold, they become convinced at this point that, as Robert Frost once penned, "there's no way out but through."

In the reinvention approach, sin and sickness are mostly dealt with as they become obstacles to the process by which a life is recreated. If guilt from the sins of poor decision-making is preventing a person from moving forward through the reinvention door, those sins are more helpfully framed as the result of a collapsing person's foiled attempt at salvaging a life that was falling apart or as a desperate person's misguided way of trying to make the pain stop. Forgiveness may be in order, but more for the lifelong resistance to listening to one's own inner voice than for the traditional failures that lie at the surface and may seem more obvious.

Clinical depression may be indicated as sickness as well. However in a reinvention approach, it is likely not primary. Helping a person move forward in his or her reinvention process may be a more effective treatment option than delving into past traumas or medical interventions. These steps are taken only as they appear as obstacles to the reinvention process.

Hopefully it is becoming clear that these two doors, restoration and reinvention, open into very different spaces. The kind of support you will seek, the professional resources you will need, the expectations you set, and the way you think about yourself, your relationships, and your future, all are different depending upon which door you choose.

Choosing Your Door

There is no simple test that will tell you which direction to go. The table below is intended to serve as a starting point for your thinking and your conversations with persons that you trust to help guide you.

Restoration	Reinvention
You view a return to your past as generally *desirable* even at great cost to yourself	You view a return to your past as generally *undesirable* and not worth the price you would have to pay with your soul
You say to yourself, *"If only I had . . . "*	You say to yourself, *"If only I could . . . "*
Aspects of your life feel painful	Your *way of life* feels painful
Your *decisions* do not reflect who you are	Your *life* does not reflect who you are
Poor *decision-making* is your biggest problem	*Fear of change* is your biggest problem
You are prepared to *make amends and rebuild trust*	You are prepared to make *decisions that may be misunderstood*
You identify more with the *prodigal son coming home*	You identify more with *Jesus at his trial*
Life as you have known it is *recoverable*	Life as you have known it is out of reach
You feel *exposed*	You feel *trapped*
You want your *life* back	You want your *soul* back
You need to get back to the *tried and true*	You need to *experiment*
You need to *learn from others*	You need to *make your own mistakes*

When we listen to real life, flesh-and-blood people talk about choosing the reinvention door, here are the kinds of things they say.

- For a person who felt like she was fighting a forest fire with a garden hose, clarity was "realizing I needed to put down the hose."

- For a person struggling to live up to the high standards of his faith community, the moment of clarity came when he said, "If this religion is about survival of the fittest, then I quit."
- For a person feeling like he was making "a thousand soul-twisting compromises" needed to keep his family relationships together, it was "I just can't do it anymore."
- For a friend left by her husband, clarity was coming to a point where she said, "I've cried long enough. I need to get up off the floor and move on with my life."
- For hundreds of other people, it is when they are able to admit, in one form or another, "It's never going to get any better . . . and that's just not good enough."

Usually it is the case that one doorway or the other resonates. It may have the quality of an undeniable truth breaking through the surface of the psyche like a tree growing through the concrete. As Elizabeth Gilbert says in her book *Eat, Pray, Love,* "I was trying not to know [that my life needed to change] but the truth kept insisting itself upon me."

Saying Four Words and the Most True Thing

Sometimes the door to take becomes clearer not by saying [or thinking] more words, but less. In cognitive behavioral therapy, it is often noted that you can tell when you have reached a core belief when you can say it in four words or less.

- I can't go back.
- Work is killing me.
- I want to die.
- My life's a lie.
- I can't go on.

Another way of discerning which door to take is to say "the most true thing." One of Michelle's personal, professional, and spiritual disciplines is a commitment to working at saying "the most true thing" possible in most situations. As she has practiced this, she has observed how twisted up our lives and our systems can become when we are *not* admitting the most true thing.

Collapse can indicate that people have lived with such terrible disconnects in their lives precisely in an attempt not to have to admit true things. "There's no going back" or "all paths forward are blocked" both can feel like admissions that are too painful to name. But the consequence of denial and resistance to what is most true is that people can end up smothered under idealistic notions of relationships and lifestyles that produce Sisyphean cycles of futile striving to fix the collapse. They can end up in cycles of abusive relationships and systems, experience soul-sucking loneliness or isolation or desperation.

Say the most true thing. You will know which door to take when those unnamed truths, that in their repression have kept you chasing your tail, are brought to light. Stared in the face. Named in their simplicity. When it is the reinvention door that you are supposed to take, it may be the first time in a long time that you have found the presence of mind to just sit still and allow the truth to trickle its way into your consciousness. It is the eye of the hurricane where skies become clear, if just for the moment. Then, it will be necessary to take a deep breath and walk through that door.

Walking through the Reinvention Door

The door is not very big; in fact, it is so narrow that you alone can pass through it. Written on the door is the word *reinvention.* On the right doorpost are the words "I matter too." On the left doorpost are the words "I let go." And over the lintel: "I am being transformed." It is the door you have chosen.

In our personal experience and years of working with people in collapse, we have found that there is one door that leads to reinvention and one door only. This may sound intransigent but we find it to be true. Jesus said that the way that leads to salvation is narrow. When this statement is generalized beyond the acceptance of a particular religious dogma to the experience of life, people find themselves brought to these narrow passages where there is a singular task to be undertaken, and nothing less will do. There are many different contradictions and many different ways that lives collapse, but there is only one doorway out that leads to reinvention.

This door is narrow. You cannot pass through it with others; you must go through alone. Fe's therapist would often listen to him about what this person did or that person said or another person thought. She would then bring him back to this question: "But, Fe Anam, what do *you* think?"

This is simply another way of saying, "I can't walk through this door for you. Will you go through it alone?"

What about the phrases on the doorposts? Walking through the reinvention door requires a person to acknowledge:

- I matter too.
- I let go.
- I am being transformed.

I Matter Too

As we've journeyed with people through reinvention, we have come to the conclusion that there is one truth that cannot be bypassed for persons in reinvention if they are to experience true clarity about where they have been and how to move forward. The reinventing person must be able to acknowledge that he or she matters. While that may seem like an obvious statement to some, to the person in reinvention, it just might be the Mount Everest of this journey.

Think of all the preparation and effort required to actually climb Mount Everest. Now imagine that mountain inside yourself, invisible except to you. Transfer all that preparation and effort of a person climbing Mount Everest to the person who needs to reach the internal summit where he or she is able to say, "I matter too." There will be no photos posted on Facebook or declarations of endurance or courage, but successfully climbing that internal mountain is every bit the lifetime achievement as Himalayan mountaineering.

Keep that image in mind. Experts say the biggest risk to Mount Everest climbers is not falling or freezing. It is altitude sickness. The human body can adapt to the thinner atmosphere, but it must do so slowly.

Many who choose reinvention will encounter a much different atmosphere on the other side of that door. It will not feel normal. Up will feel like down. Thinking, speaking, and acting as if "I matter too" may feel strange and disorienting. Like the climbers of that external Mount Everest, it will take time to adjust.

Our experience with people who find themselves in this situation is that they tend to be those who have spent a lifetime deceiving themselves into believing that they have no responsibility for their own well-being. Whether this tendency was from the experiences of childhood, low self-esteem, or reinforcement of behaviors that got one attention or esteem in return for abandoning oneself, we don't feel the need to identify causality to recognize the truth of our vast antidotal experience. When we find people at the point of collapse in their lives, they have often been working tirelessly to live in a way that is least disruptive to anyone else. They have spent years making decisions, building careers, and forming identities around what was working for other people while taking little or no responsibility for their own physical, emotional, and spiritual health.

"If I am not for myself, who will be? If I am not for others, what am I?" This rabbibical tenet from Mishna of Hillel offers a profound insight—I have a responsibility for my well-being that I cannot delegate to others.

It sounds noble to say, "I don't matter. Serving others is what really counts." However if we say what is most true, what we really mean is that we assume an unspoken deal: "I will sacrifice myself for the needs of others, but I expect others will do the same for me." This implicit contract usually remains unspoken until collapse painfully exposes it as a charade. If your health falls apart because you are working sixty hours a week in a job without adequate rest and stress management, the job will not nurse you back to physical, emotional, and spiritual health. You will have to do that. If you find yourself clinically depressed because you are in a family system where members focus all their anxiety on you, those family members will not help you set the boundaries that are crucial to your well-being. You will have to do that.

One nonnegotiable part of reinvention is the clarity of the realization that "I matter enough to take responsibility for myself *even when it costs other people.*" In Michelle's clinical practice, she has seen this emerging truth working to be born for people, creating the kind of pain only experienced in childbirth. The examples are legion: A mother concluding that she needs to sell her small business because the work feels empty, even with no other income prospects and the real likelihood that her children will need to move out of their large home and into an urban apartment. A husband saying to his wife, "I can't leave my community of support and move with you clear across the country in order for you to follow your dreams."

Each of these examples could be read as stubbornness or selfishness on the part of the reinventor. But there is nothing noble about living with unspoken expectations of others only to self-destruct when those needs are not met. How will the world benefit from your mission if your failure to say "I matter too" leads not only to collapse but into the darker realms of self-destructive behaviors or even suicide? Persons in reinvention eventually begin to understand what some others may never understand: they are in this spot precisely because the easiest thing for them to do has always been to abandon themselves. The hardest thing for them to do—the climb up Mt. Everest—is to matter enough to give priority to the inner drive toward vitality that is welling up inside them.

Our experience often tells us that for the victims of domestic violence in faith communities, their inclination to stay stuck in an abusive collapse is often buttressed by the perception that the *life* of Jesus didn't matter, only his selfless death. However if that were true, the angel wouldn't have warned his father to flee to Egypt with the infant Jesus. He would have left him to be slaughtered by Herod. When the crowd tried to throw Jesus over a cliff, he found a way to escape, not something he would have worried about if he didn't believe that his life mattered. One could argue that Jesus needed to stay alive to fulfill his mission, but don't all people also have a mission?

Jesus took steps to insure his physical safety, but also his emotional well-being. He refused to spend time with those who spoke of him in degrading ways. He gathered around himself a social network of both men and women who were supportive. When John the Baptist was thrown into prison, Jesus did not offer to join him. In fact the tendency of Jesus to engage in feasting rather than the austere lifestyle of John the Baptist led some to question the validity of his mission. Repeatedly, when these expressions of "I matter too" in the life of Jesus are pointed out to the victims of domestic violence, a great burden rolls off their shoulders.

I Let Go

No ship can set sail when it is anchored at port. What keeps people stuck and thwarts reinvention is what they hold onto.

There is a well-known story about a young child who had her hand stuck in a very expensive vase. The frantic mother tried everything she knew to remove it: soap, olive oil, and running hot water over the neck of the vase. After an hour of trying, she reluctantly covered her child's face with a towel and broke the vase with a hammer. It became immediately apparent why the child's hand was stuck; her hand was formed as a fist. Slowly she opened it to reveal . . . a coin. A beautiful vase had been destroyed in order to hold onto a penny.

Most people who have found themselves at this point in their reinvention have spent an extraordinary amount of time, emotional energy, and resources attempting to hold their life or someone else's life together. They have taken out loans to cover the credit card debt of a spouse that won't stop spending. They have gone to counseling. They have stayed in jobs that are killing them. They have taken second jobs or even third jobs. Even if their lives have not changed outwardly the mental and emotional labor they engage inwardly to try to make life work can be more oppressive than a difficult boss.

These people are generally exhausted by various expenditures, frustrated by the lack of impact those expenditures seem to have had on making things better, and are desperate because they've tried everything they know to do. But clarity is the moment in the fullness of time that allows the truth to find its way to the surface.

- Life as I know it is over.
- No amount of spending will allow us to keep up with the Joneses.
- What's happening to me is abusive and it's got to stop.
- I will never be able to "fix" the person I want to fix.
- The community I am in will never accept me for who I am.

These are all various ways of talking about relinquishment. This is the acknowledgement that the I-35W Mississippi River Bridge could not have been held together with duct tape. That some relationships can't be saved. That the best thing I can do is put down the garden hose and let this forest fire . . . or reputation . . . or relationship . . . or profession burn.

Anxiety about a vocational change is one thing that keeps people stuck. Research shows that men and women who take a new job after age fifty will experience an average pay cut of 14 percent. These men and women who are reinventing their vocational lives may have to let go of the expectations that they will make as much money in their reinvented lives. On the other hand, many people who are paying attention to their own gifts and motivations may end up doing far better financially by avoiding the high physical, emotional, relational, and spiritual costs of living a life that is in a perpetual state of collapse. Jesus put it this way: "What shall a man [or woman] give in [exchange] for his [or her] soul?" (Matt. 16:26, ESV).

Pulling up the anchor and letting go is a terrifying prospect because it admits the powerlessness with which most people live, but that they resist most of the time. But for a reinventor, while terrifying, this recognition is also a giant sigh of relief. It is cold water to a soul that has been parched. It is deep sleep for someone who has been wide-awake for days on end. It is relief from the backbreaking labor of building sandbag walls to keep the flood waters of truth at bay. As terrifying as letting go might be, it also resonates deeply with a reinventor's soul.

Already Dead and Yet Alive for the First Time

The apostle Paul's teaching in the New Testament can be helpful. "I have been crucified with Christ and I no longer live" (Gal. 2:20, NIV). Many people have core beliefs that govern their understanding of what it means to be alive.

- I can't take being fired or losing my job.
- I can't handle being rejected, misunderstood, or losing my reputation.
- I can't live without my family members.
- I can't change my lifestyle or reduce my standard of living.

Paul's insight is simply this: I have already died. The worst has already happened to me. What I have always feared has already come to pass. People can no longer manipulate or emotionally blackmail a corpse. They cannot insult, reject, misunderstand, dismiss, impoverish, or abandon it.

As strange as this may sound, this perspective is extremely liberating. Corpses can't fix things. They can't make other people happy, proud, or forgiving. During Fe's collapse when just about everything had fallen apart around him, he would say to himself, "Fe, you are already dead. It doesn't matter. Let it go."

In spite of a soaring economy, rising employment, and falling homelessness, Korea is considered the suicide capital of the world. The nonsuicidal citizens are baffled, and in a bid to solve this puzzle, a bizarre movement has sprung up with the hopes that giving people a little taste of death will restore their will to live.

It's called the "Well Dying" or "Near Death" movement. It involves fake funeral services. A philosophical guru lectures them for a bit and then has them write their own eulogies. They then climb inside a coffin and meditate for half an hour.

Strange as it seems to those who are nonsuicidal, this experience is liberating. One suicidal dentist and fake funeral enthusiast explained, "All I want to be is a good father. However, there is so much competition; I was under a lot of stress. Waking up each morning and living each day felt too painful. I was looking for something that would soothe and heal my mind. When I was inside that coffin, I felt like the weight of all my worries was lifted."

You may not have to climb into a coffin to experience relinquishment, but finding a way to offer grace to yourself as you let go is crucial. Perhaps you have noticed that folks at funerals offer a remarkable degree of grace to the deceased. Those who were considered rebellious while living suddenly are described as "free-spirited." Those who were stubborn are now "determined." Those who were cantankerous in life are now "outspoken" in death. When it was thought that Tom Sawyer and Huck Finn had died, Mark Twain's funeral preacher "related many a touching incident in the lives of the departed, too, which illustrated their sweet, generous natures, and the people could easily see, now, how noble and beautiful those episodes were, and remembered with grief that at the time they occurred they had seemed rank rascalities, well deserving of the cowhide" (from *The Adventures of Tom Sawyer*). The dead find grace that eludes the living.

The paradox, of course, is that you have died without having physically died at all. Death is a relinquishment that makes a more abundant life possible, life that is vibrant and authentic, life that has the capacity to make a contribution to the world. In fact adopting a perspective of a death that has already taken place may be the best way to avoid a real death: suicide.

I Am Being Transformed

When we ask ourselves, "What experiences seem to produce significant human transformation?" we can't help but notice that they aren't things like Easter and Christmas Eve extravaganzas in spite of the inordinate amount of energy clergy types faithfully put into them. Instead, on the list of things that do make a transformational difference, we see:

- Near death experiences
- Recovery from addiction
- Short-term mission work
- Deep and meaningful relationships

The common thread of these experiences is that none of them is manufacturable and all of them contain factors that are coming from outside oneself. While persons can choose whether or not to go on a short-term mission trip, pursue a soul friend whose path they cross, or attend AA meetings, those choices are only part of the story. The other part of the story—the divine part . . . the nebulous part—is the part where they find themselves caught up in this river of "something" that carries them along. They may, with fear and trepidation, name that to be God. Others might disagree, in fact some probably will. Often a significant crisis for reinventors can be precisely that while they are experiencing transformation, those around them aren't able to see it. Fe once said to his therapist, "It seems like everyone thinks I am losing my faith . . ." and then she completed the sentence, "at the very moment you are finding it." "Yes," he exclaimed. "That's it!"

No doubt, you must do the hard work of claiming your own soul and relinquishment. This work can be laborsome, painstaking, and energy depleting. But for the person standing at the door of reinvention, there is something happening *to* him or her as well. The work of "I matter too" and "I let go" does not fuel the reinvention as much as it protects what is already happening, helping the person not to abandon this thing that seems wild and uncontrollable, and feels unexplainable but compelling. In truth one can't do much to create it. However in order to fully reinvent, one must be responsive to it and participate with it.

Steps to Take in the Clarity Stage

If you are at this point of clarity and choose to walk through the reinvention door, here is what we recommend.

In addition to continuing to see your reinvention therapist, find a spiritual director who can understand reinvention, transformation, and who has the capacity to journey with you into potentially unconventional places.

Do the following exercise developed by the psychotherapist Lawrence LeShan.

Suppose your Fairy Godmother will come in that door in a few minutes. She will make you an offer. In six months your inner and outer life can be exactly what you would like it to be so that you would use yourself most completely and have the maximum enjoyment and zest possible. You can change your feelings and your circumstances. There are no limitations on age, sex, education, and so forth. We shall assume good physical health. There are only two catches. You must tell her in the next five minutes, and this is a once-in-a-lifetime deal. She won't be back after granting your proposal. . . ."[1]

Once you have done that, you will have just described your heart's deepest desire and where and how you would love to live. Now take action.

Begin to journal the most true things you can. Then compare them to the doorposts. Reflect on how many of your true things are related to the doorposts of "I matter," "I let go," and "I am being transformed."

Process that with your therapist.

COMMITMENT

Commitment is the grit and the guts of reinvention. It presses you to try and accomplish more than you thought you were capable of. It opens up new vistas and horizons.

In 1996 Fe strapped a parachute on his back and jumped out of a plane flying at five thousand feet. It was nothing like he thought it would be. He had imagined the plane door would be opened and he would dive head first into the open sky. Instead, his jumpmaster instructed him to actually step out of the plane onto the wheel strut with his hands holding onto the diagonal wing strut. He then had to slide his hands outward on the wing strut to get his body as far away from the fuselage of the plane as possible and pick up his feet so that his body was blowing in the wind like a sheet on a clothesline.

Fe still remembers the last thing the instructor said, "Once you step out of this plane, it would be unsafe to let you back in. You will only have one way to the ground: falling."

That is commitment.

Once you pass through the door of clarity, there is only one path to reinvention: your own commitment. Everyone's commitment is different. There will be different paths for different persons climbing up the mountain, but the goal is the same: to significantly alter your patterns of living in a way that will expand your zest for life and capacity to contribute to the world.

Making Commitment Real in Your Life

As we have studied successful reinventors, we have observed a number of elements of their commitment.

First, be your own Thomas Edison. Think of your life as a laboratory where you are in charge and new discoveries are made on a daily basis. Therapists, spiritual directors, coaches, and supportive friends are invaluable aids. But at the end of the day, only you can make the investments that reinvention will require; only you will hold the patent on the lessons you have learned and the person you have become.

Lauren, a person whose reinvention led her out of a highly structured religious community, did the messy, fumbling work of learning in adulthood how to buy pants and how to get a haircut for the first time in her life. In reflecting on that experience she says, "If I could change one thing, I wish I would have had a friend who could have taught me how to do those things. But it was exciting to test my individual strength to see if I could learn to survive in a different universe. Everything I knew was turned upside down. It was both a crushing, alienating time and an exhilarating time. But I doubt I will ever again feel as alive as I did then."

Second, show up. Reinvention is an opportunity to bring what you love into the mix of your life. It is critical that you allow those parts of you to finally show up. At this point in the reinvention process there is little excuse left for a dreary routine of uninspired tasks while what you love is left waiting in the wings. Collapse has left you with little to lose.

Complete this simple sentence: I love . . . Think about how you can allow that thing you love to show up in your life. Then repeat. Identify three things you love and ways that those parts of yourself can show up in your life.

One of the ways Fe would complete that sentence is, "I love to think about things from a different perspective." He had always felt the need to critique that part of himself, turn down the volume, and hold it in check. Only during his reinvention did he finally allow it to fully show up in his life. He also loves bringing ideas into reality and leaving a mark on the world. Making the commitment that these three loves will show up every day has been a critical aspect of his reinvention.

Make the commitment that what you love will show up in your life.

Third, take the long view. In our strategic planning work with organizations, we have come to learn that something is strategic if 1) it can't be done quickly,

2) it can't be done alone, and 3) once it is done it is difficult to undo. Building a new facility, for example, fits all three criteria.

Achieving happiness is also a strategic goal. If you are an unhappy person, there may be little you can do in the short run to turn yourself into a happy person. Over time, with the right shifts in your own soul and a little help from friends, you can develop a life characterized by joy and gratitude. Once you find that way of living, you develop what we call a Timex spirituality: you can take a licking and keep on ticking.

Reinvention is a strategic goal, often measured in years. We're guessing even reading that sentence may scare some of you, but here's the thing. Years come to us in an accumulation of minutes; as the old expression goes, "How do you eat an elephant? One bite at a time." One person in reinvention found that the only way to stay sane was to live four minutes at a time. The clinical world calls this mindfulness, and it means grounding oneself in the present. When people get caught up in the past, they can spiral into regret and despair. When they get too far into the future, they can get so far ahead of themselves that they get overwhelmed and become paralyzed by the obstacles in front of them. But as is often spoken in the AA rooms, the overall task of commitment is to try to do "the next right thing." The task is not to the next twelve right things. Just do the next right thing in the next four minutes.

Fourth, put everything on the table. For persons in commitment, every-thing—all the nonnegotiables—need to be on the table in order to be as creative as reinvention may require. When people get stuck, the narrative is often the same. They try to imagine how to move forward, but the only options on the table are the ones that basically allow everything in their lives to stay intact. They try to think about how to get out of an impossible work situation without having to alter their standard of living, impact their family members, or say what they really think to people who really need to hear it. As Henry Ford noted, the results are predictable: "If you always do what you've always done, you'll always get what you've always got."

Line up all the sacred cows of your life for assessment. The freedom to do this will fuel the imagination in a way that will help you think outside of the normal categories of behavior and solutions. This could mean selling a home in order to quit a job that is soul sucking. A married couple might decide to have a commuter relationship for a time so that both people can get their needs met when those needs exist in different geographical regions. It might mean putting boundaries on your adult children, knowing that they will likely alienate themselves from you, requiring you to create a new family of support.

Fe moved into some friends' basement and slept on a sleeper sofa for three years, saying, "I would rather live in someone's basement and eat Ramen noodles than sell my soul." This gave him the freedom to strategically create services that didn't previously exist for libraries, churches, and other organizations. It also enabled him to write his first book on pastoral transitions. He says that while externally it looked like he was "down and out," the incredible generosity of friends combined with a willingness to adopt a very modest lifestyle laid the foundation for his entire reinvention and future happiness.

When it comes to commitment, your choices are only as limited as your imagination and your courage.

Fifth, get creative. Hundreds of books, scores of workshops, and gigabits of information have focused on the development of creativity. Here's our favorite definition of creativity: creativity is bringing together two things that have never, or rarely, been put together before. The genius of Gutenberg's printing press was simply that it put together the mechanism of a winepress with the flexibility of movable type.

It is nothing new to say that everyone has gifts. Combining those gifts in an original way is creative.

Psychologist Lawrence LeShan tells the story of a gang member in New York who came to see him in search of a different future. After listening carefully, LeShan observed that he was physically strong and loved the thrill of facing a life-threatening crisis. A high school sophomore could have made similar observations. LeShan took it one step further. He put together those two attributes and concluded that the young man would make an excellent firefighter. After all, firefighters need to be strong and love the thrill of facing a life-threatening crisis (after which they sit around and boast of their exploits)! And that's exactly what the young man did. He went on to become a successful firefighter.

Creativity doesn't require that you become an artist or composer. Creativity is expressed in the original way that you combine the different elements of your life to make a life worth living.

Sixth, experiment. This is your opportunity to try on different "lives" to see how they fit. Michelle quit her job and spent a year living in a conservative

Mennonite community in Brooklyn, teaching science to underprivileged eighth graders. She said to the pastor of the community, "I'll throw myself into the life of this community and give it a try. But I'm probably going to cry a lot. And question a lot. I won't hold back either of those things, but if you can handle it, so can I." She didn't hold back.

She wore long skirts and a bonnet on her head and stopped cutting her hair, all of which felt unusual, experimental, and creative. It didn't last forever. Her journey eventually parted ways with the Mennonites and led her to a Presbyterian seminary. But she made great friends, learned an extraordinary amount about God and herself, and counts it among the most transformative experiences of her life.

Approaching life as an experiment allows you to turn "failures" into learning experiences without punishing yourself into a self-defeating paralysis. Thomas Edison tested 10,000 substances for the filament of an electric light bulb before he found one that both worked and was economically viable. That means he failed 9,999 times.

It's possible that you as a reinventor have spent most of your life not failing at things. In fact it's even likely that the desire not to fail and to avoid rejection is partly how you got here in the first place. An expectation that you will be good at everything you try—that projects will always succeed, and that outcomes will always make you look good and win the favor and support of those around you—will set you up for disappointment that can deflate your reinvention. But an expectation that failure *will* be a part of what you do will normalize the hurdles in a way that will fuel your ability to get over them.

In the rapidly changing environment of today's world, businesses are being told that if they are not making mistakes they are not learning fast enough. This is simply because what worked yesterday will not work today, and the only way to discover what will work today is to experiment. The same can be said about any reinventor. You know your life of yesterday no longer works. The only way to discover what will work is to give yourself permission to both succeed and fail.

One reinventor told us that when he was most anxious about failing, he would hear a voice in his head that would say, "You have spent your whole life achieving modest goals with guaranteed success. For once in your life, do something worth failing at!"

Seventh, take action. Sometimes you can't think yourself into a new way of acting. You have to act yourself into a new way of thinking.

Studies show that simply putting a smile on your face, even when you don't feel like it, can make you happier. In fact it seems that anything that puts a smile on your face can make you happier! A 2009 issue of *Scientific American* reports a study of women who had received frown-inhibiting Botox injections that found they were happier and less anxious than the general population![1]

This is not a phenomenon that is unfamiliar. If people waited to do the laundry until they felt like it, they would all be walking around in dirty clothes. The expression "fake it till you make it" is used in everything from business to AA to describe the process of going through the motions when your heart is not in it.

Behavior theory says that feelings will follow behaviors as behaviors produce successes, something we refer to as "spiraling up." But before that can happen, sometimes the reinventor needs to do things he or she doesn't want to do. Go jogging when you would rather stay in bed. Apply for the job you aren't sure you're qualified for. Take the risk when you're scared as hell.

Eighth, build a community. Part of reinvention will likely require releasing some people from responsibility for a relationship with you. But find those people and communities who will validate, support, and be invested in your reinvention creativity. This will often mean finding brand new communities that didn't exist in your former life. It could mean finding new dimensions to old friendships that you had underestimated. It might mean that some people move into your inner circle and some people move out of it.

Ninth, watch for signs that you are receiving spiritual help for your reinvention process. A quote from Goethe says it well:

> Until one is committed, there is hesitancy, the chance to draw back—Concerning all acts of initiative (and creation), there is one elementary truth, the ignorance of which kills countless ideas and splendid plans: that the moment one definitely commits oneself, then Providence moves too. All sorts of things occur to help one that would never otherwise have occurred. A whole stream of events issues from the decision, raising in one's favor all manner of unforeseen incidents, meetings and material assistance, which no man could have dreamed would have come his way. Whatever

you can do, or dream you can do, begin it. Boldness has genius, power, and magic in it. Begin it now.[2]

Commitment is the part of the process where reinventors are most likely to get stuck. Rather than address all those areas here, we have created "Getting Unstuck," Part Two of this book. You may want to skim through those pages to get help for the particular areas that tend to hang you up.

More Steps to Take in the Commitment Stage

If you are in the commitment phase, here is what we suggest.

1. It is important not to try to do this alone. While the universe will come to your aid, you will also face a degree of resistance in your creative endeavors that will challenge you and try your resolve. This is the point in the process when you should be actively investing in relationships that are resonant with your reinvention. Pay attention to who the creative people are in your life. Listen for affirmation from those who are excited and encouraging about what you are doing and becoming. Learn to lean on them. Befriend them. Invest in them.

2. Set your expectations such that while you have some large and overarching goals, you have other goals and dreams that are smaller and more bite-sized. Fast successes will contribute to your confidence, which will encourage you to take bigger risks over time.

3. Are you still seeing your therapist-turned-reinvention coach? Good.

4. Keep a list of your reinvention successes. Know where to find it when you start to forget how far you've come. Look at it at those times.

5. When you start to feel stuck, do something. Often people can develop analysis paralysis. Sometimes too much thinking is the problem and an action in any direction can remove the blockage. Trust that even if it's wrong, you will have what it takes to make it right.

6. Get a good book on mindfulness and start practicing mindfulness techniques. We recommend *Mindfulness—An Eight-Week Plan for Finding Peace in a Frantic World*, by Mark Williams and Danny Penman or *A Mindfulness-Based Stress Reduction Workbook* by Bob Stahl and Elisha Goldstein, which comes with a CD loaded with guided meditations.

7. Get a good book on family systems theory and read it. We recommend *The Eight Concepts of Bowen Theory* by Roberta M. Gilbert.

5

COHERENCE

The primary difference between the light emitted by a laser and that produced by a household lightbulb is that laser light is coherent. Coherence is just another way of saying that all the light waves from a laser beam are moving in step with one another.

Coherence makes a huge difference in the power of light. A single, 100-watt bulb can barely light a small room. A single, 100-watt coherent laser beam can be used to cut metal.

Coherence is the place where meaning is made, values are solidified, and practices are put in place to reinforce the fullness of one's reinvented self. It is what gives the reinvented life its power and capacity. This is part of what enabled Jesus to focus the spiritual capacity of his life on the needs of others. Up to this point, reinvention has been largely a self-focused process. Not selfish. Not self-indulgent. It has simply been focused on the self. But remember that the goal of the reinvented life is not simply self-survival. The goal is to significantly enhance one's zest for living and expand one's contribution to the world, and do so in a way that is sustainable.

By the time people reach this part of the reinvention process, they have come a long way from the agony and chaos that characterized collapse. For those in collapse, this chapter might seem like a fantasy so distant from where they are as to feel like a pipe dream. If that describes you, we suggest that you postpone reading this chapter until you are closer to its reality. Others in collapse might experience this chapter as a light at the end of the tunnel that offers vision and hope. We leave the timing to your best judgment.

We believe that developing coherence is the essential final step in the reinvention process. It is tempting to stop the process at the end of the commitment phase. The pain that served as motivation for reinvention is largely gone, but the goal of reinvention is the beginning of joy not the end of pain. As a reinventor emerges from the commitment phase and all the creativity it has required, a new normal has taken hold. It feels good to be alive again. But if a person stops there, he or she runs the risk of returning to a perpetual state of contraction.

Brad was an ordained minister who reinvented his life theologically and vocationally. He had been a minister but could no longer believe the claims of his ordination vows. He left ministry and found a job that gave him a sense of meaning and purpose that was far more aligned with his reinvented self. Still, he maintained his ordination so as not to be disruptive. He convinced himself that it wouldn't hurt anything to keep it because he knew who he was and what he believed. But Brad found himself increasingly uncomfortable that his outward status did not match his inner infrastructure. Following his commitment phase, he should have felt alive in a new way. But this nagging connection to his old self caused him to experience such contradiction and inner conflict that he could barely enjoy his new identity. It was several years later when Brad finally rescinded his ordination that he identifies as the completed circle of his reinvention.

Coherence is defined in Webster's online dictionary as the "integration of diverse elements, relationships, or values." We define coherence as bringing the various aspects of life into alignment with the reinvented self.

These various aspects of life are extensive and finding coherence in them requires intentionality. Passivity related to the reconstruction of your higher ideals will not get you there. Purposefully holding areas of your life up to the light for scrutiny, evaluation, and modification is required.

Questions to explore coherence and community

- In what places do I thrive?
- Where and with whom will I live?

- What kind of environment spurs my creativity and effectiveness?
- What will be my relationship with place and community?
- What environments optimize my capacity to contribute? How do I identify and connect with these?
- In what environments will I starve?
- What environment will block my capacity to contribute? How do I identify and avoid these?

The Lessons of a Trip Home

Jesus had to wrestle with these questions when he returned to his hometown, as recorded in the Gospel of Mark. It is worth citing this text in its entirety.

> He left that place and came to his hometown, and his disciples followed him. On the sabbath he began to teach in the synagogue, and many who heard him were astounded. They said, "Where did this man get all this? What is this wisdom that has been given to him? What deeds of power are being done by his hands! Is not this the carpenter, the son of Mary and brother of James and Joses and Judas and Simon, and are not his sisters here with us?" And they took offense at him. Then Jesus said to them, "Prophets are not without honor, except in their hometown, and among their own kin, and in their own house." And he could do no deed of power there, except that he laid his hands on a few sick people and cured them. And he was amazed at their unbelief (6:1–5, NRSV).

What happens to Jesus in Capernaum convinces him once and for all that he cannot stay there. It also offers valuable insight into the ways that a community, which is not aligned with reinvented persons, can rob them of the fruits of all their hard work.

Lesson 1. In a community that is not coherent with reinvention, reinventors may always be defined by what they were in their past instead of by what they are becoming. Even though Jesus demonstrated an incredible power in his reinvented life, his community could not resist seeing him simply as the carpenter.

Lesson 2. In a community that is not coherent with reinvention, conversations may always gravitate toward family relationships instead of purpose and mission.

Those relationships may be backward looking as in the case of Jesus: "Is this not . . . the son of Mary?" Or they may become so focused on the next generations as parents live vicariously, and sometimes parasitically, upon the heroic feats of children and grandchildren.

Lesson 3. In a community that is not coherent with reinvention, reinventors' capabilities may be confined to those that are familiar and comfortable for others. Anything more will be criticized and even punished as prideful. "Where did this man get all this?"

Lesson 4. In a community that is not coherent with reinvention, the impact of the lessons named above may deaden reinventors' inner zest. Their capacity to offer something special to the world may be so greatly diminished that they feel like they were never reinvented at all. Jesus could do no mighty work there. Neither will reinventors.

Lesson 5. In a community that is not coherent with reinvention, even having a great support group may not be enough to keep reinventors afloat emotionally and spiritually. Jesus had his twelve disciples with him, but he still found himself being pulled under by the broader social context of the community he had chosen to reenter.

Finding Relationships Where We Can Thrive

This example about Jesus returning to his hometown reminds us that we must think carefully about our environment. In the biological realm, we have numerous examples that can serve as helpful metaphors. Adult frogs share few features in common with their tailed, legless antecedents, yet they are the same creature. Jellyfish begin as polyps usually devoid of locomotion and the characteristic long jellyfish tentacles. The radical difference between caterpillars and their subsequent butterfly stage has often been used as a symbol of human transformation. What human beings, butterflies, and a host of other creatures have in common when they reinvent is that they thrive in different environments on the other side of reinvention. Caterpillars do well in environments with nutrients that are accessible by crawling. Butterflies do well in environments with nutrients that are accessible by flying. Butterflies naturally develop coherence as they choose to frequent environments rich in nectar.

As a Second Day person, people often ask Fe if he worries about falling back into suicidal thinking. His answer is always the same. "I have to be vigilant over my own thinking." Yet there is another answer that he always keeps to himself. "I am a butterfly. I have to stay where people treat me like I can fly instead of like a worm."

Questions to explore coherence and relationships

- Who are the people who nourish your soul and how do you invest in them?
- Is there toxicity in your relationships that needs to be named and eradicated for the health of your soul?
- With whom will you share your heart?
- What role will family play in the formation of your reinvented identity?
- In what way does your definition of family need to be redefined?

One of Michelle's reinvention commitments is to "practice stickiness" in relationships. That means following up with concrete steps when a gesture of relationship is extended. That means articulating her desire to be friends overtly and clearly when chemistry emerges. That means asking people out to lunch and saying yes when people do the same. There can be a great deal of passive rejection with this practice as many, if not most, offers go nowhere. But living sticky is as much for her own coherence as for any other relational outcomes that it might produce. Michelle says, "I never want to be the reason that a friendship doesn't happen." Being sticky is her commitment to herself. It is a coherent way of working towards the relational life she desires.

On the flip side of that, relational traps can sabotage coherence to the extent that one is unwilling to redefine family or bracket off toxic relational interactions when that is needed. In Jesus' reinvented life, he did the same when he said, "These [disciples] are my mother and my brothers" (Luke 8:21, Aramaic Bible). While it sounds harsh, Jesus understood a challenging reinvention truth: sometimes family needs to be redefined.

Many reinventing people have had to build a family from scratch when they concluded that their own families would not or could not support their reinvented self. A commitment to and an investment in reinvention families is contrary to common cultural expectations of familial obligation and primacy. But coherence requires that our energies be invested where and with whom we can flourish.

Developing Symbols of Our New Identity

Symbols provide a compact, visual representation of what we value, who we are, and a rehearsal of important elements of our story. One possibility for developing coherence is creating a symbol that represents the reinvented self.

Fe was deep in the collapse phase when a symbol began to emerge in his journaling. It consisted of two parabolas facing outward, and three intersecting straight lines. He named it the Magi symbol. The Magi symbol represents Fe's:

- View of the universe consisting of two complementary perspectives, sensory and spiritual.
- View of eternity as an ever-expanding, infinite quest.
- View of the integration of math, art, and science.
- Commitment to Christianity.
- Aspirations to a life of wisdom lived at the intersections.

As Fe was emerging from the commitment phase of reinvention and the clouds were beginning to clear, he started using the symbol after his signature to reinforce the new understanding of himself. He had note cards made with the Magi symbol on the front. His wedding ring holds the symbol. He painted the symbol on his laptop computer, and his daughter even made him a canvas Magi grocery bag!

Not everyone might create his or her own symbol. But many people have acquired meaningful tattoos as a representation of their reinvention. Project Semicolon is one example. The semicolon as a symbol represents a place where an author could have put a period but instead chose to keep going after a pause. Started in 2013 by someone who was grieving the death of her father by suicide, this movement has gone viral. Thousands of people have now tattooed the semicolon on their wrist as a reminder to themselves and the world that their story is not over.

Michelle has come to identify the tree of life as her symbol. This symbol has deep meaning for her as it:

- Gives expression to arms that stretch wide and roots that go deep.
- Is reflective of her Christian identity while embracing a broader spirituality.
- Sings of her connection to the earth and the ruggedness of her journey.
- Can provide shelter in its branches and relief in shade due to its hard-won stability and maturity.

A quick scan around Michelle's life will reveal the tree of life in her jewelry, her wall hangings, the mantle art work in her home; it is even the center of the logo for the organization she directs. She didn't come up with it; it's a very common symbol. But it is the symbol that has come to give coherence to her reinvention.

Rituals and Reinvention

Rituals serve a similar purpose as a symbol. For many reinventors, the rituals and myths around which their life was built prior to reinvention have been lost. New ones need to take their place. Michelle's husband wrote a family food prayer that is unique to them, expressing their family's theological hopes when they could find no such prayer that they could live with. That daily ritual has become part of the family's meaning making as they name together who they are and what they choose to be about.

> *Life within us, love between us, joining us as one*
> *With soil and air and living things, with water and with sun.*
> *Make us hopeful, make us faithful, make us know our worth*
> *Helping others in their need and caring for your earth.*

Vocation and Reinvention

Research shows that hating your job has serious consequences that can undo the positive effects of reinvention. These effects include damage to relationships, lowering your immune system, and increasing the risk of serious disease.

Questions to explore coherence and vocation

- What work is resonant to you?
- If your former job is no longer an option, how will you support yourself and those for whom you are responsible?
- What are the vocational compromises you can make and still be whole?
- What are the vocational compromises you cannot make?

One reinventor, Tom, concluded that giving up his family business, which offered him freedom and financial security, was necessary in order to be mentored in his craft. Vocational isolation had caused his collapse, and he needed a community that would teach him, hold him accountable, and "be in it with him" more than he needed independence. For Tom, that vocation shift was coherence. For Jimmy, his stable job with a construction company was the safe way to go, but he had always dreamed of being a cabinet maker. Starting his own company allowed him to create and live out his dream of owning his own business in spite of the financial risks. For Jimmy, that was coherence. Nicole left a high-paying corporate job in banking to volunteer in nursing homes. She stated, "I would rather do what I love for free than to hate what I do for money." Knowing what one *can* give up to have what one *cannot* give up is the key to vocational coherence.

Spirituality, Finances, and Mission

In our busy, overly full lives, carving out times for grounding and spiritual connection require intentionality. As part of his reinvention, Brian, an introverted pastor, learned that following Sunday morning worship, he needed to spend the afternoon in the woods finding his grounding again. With small children at home, that was a major family commitment but one that transformed his personal life, his family life, and his ministry. That act of coherence connected him to God and to the earth.

Many people on the other side of reinvention find faith communities that are places where they can thrive, where ideals are taught that they can support, and where community members embrace them. Still others find that they are no longer able to participate in their faith community like they once did.

Neither one nor the other is right or wrong. The coherence question is whether or not your new beliefs, values, and ideals are being lived out in meaningful ways through your engagement or lack thereof with a faith community.

Questions to explore faith and spirituality

- What beliefs about God am I willing to articulate and offer?
- Will I attend worship and if so where?
- If not, what will I incorporate in my life that grounds me in that which I experience as ultimate?
- What will be my relationship with the earth?

As Jesus said so well, "Where your treasure is, there will your heart be also" (Matt. 6:21, KJV). A coherent life cannot avoid or ignore the realities of money.

These are not just questions about how much you give to charity. Financial coherence is about investing in that world that you hope to leave behind. It means forward thinking related to who you want to become. Some people invest their resources in travel instead of real estate. Some invest theirs in education instead of retirement accounts. Some give to one global mission. Others give when their friends ask it of them. There is no right answer to how and to whom you give. Coherence just requires that you consider the questions.

Questions to explore financial issues

- How will I spend my money in ways that are resonant with my reinvented self?
- What are the values, ethics, and goals that drive my financial choices?

Again, we look to Jesus as a model of what a coherent life, lived with missional commitment, looks like. But he is not the only one. Henri Nouwen, a highly renowned author, theologian, and scholar held positions at both Yale and Harvard but ultimately found his truest mission by leaving academia to live in community with those with intellectual disabilities. As Fredrick Buechner has said, one's calling "is the place where your deep gladness and the world's deep hunger meet" (from *Wishful Thinking: A Theological ABC*). Often that capacity for contribution is only possible on the other side of reinvention.

Questions to explore ethics and mission

- What is right, wrong, and what is the scale of values that informs whether I will fight, object, withdraw, or simply sigh and keep drinking my coffee?
- What do I want to accomplish in the world?
- What is my capacity for contribution that matches my desire?

There are other questions of coherence as well. Questions of physical and emotional health. Questions of pleasure and beauty. Questions related to how to spend one's time, parent children, and carry oneself in the world.

When all of these parts of one's life and experience are brought into alignment, new possibilities emerge that previously could scarcely be imagined. Doors begin to open to doors that then open to more doors. The reinventor begins to realize that the new person he or she has become offers new opportunities for growth, relationships, and service as various aspects of life are brought under the reinvention spell.

In coherence, the reinventor discovers capacities, relationships, and opportunities not considered possible before reinvention, when he or she was in a mode of simple survival. When Thomas Edison invented the electric light, he had a fairly limited application in mind: illuminating homes. When the railroad tycoon Henry Villard approached Edison to have his lighting system installed on a steamboat, he was initially resistant to the idea. The inventor himself had to open up to the many capacities of what he had invented.

Likewise, the New Testament makes it clear that Jesus emerged from his reinvention with powers he did not exhibit previously. There is no suggestion that Jesus could have stayed in Capernaum, worked as a carpenter, had weekly Sabbath dinners with his family, and still run a healing and teaching ministry on the side. (As will be presented later in the book, there is good evidence to the contrary.) God used Jesus' reinvention process to imbue Jesus with capacities that he had to discover and learn to use.

In the coherence stage, a reinventor develops powerful gifts to offer the world that previously lay dormant beneath the short-circuiting effects of contradiction or the rubble of collapse. Many of the persons that walked away during collapse now return, except now they return not to a person who is pretending, devastated, or even suicidal, but to one who has something more to offer.

The choice to reinvent your life is a choice that no one else can make. The joy that comes from reinvention is a joy that no one else can take.

More Steps to Take in the Coherence Stage

If you are in the coherence stage, here is what we recommend.

1. Pay attention to the possible emergence of a symbol for your life. Observe and practice what feels like the development of rituals. Write a mission statement for who you will purpose to be. Any of these are ways to give voice and expression to your reinvented self.

2. Consider what possibilities your reinvented self has yet to explore. Allow your imagination to consider what once felt impossible. Journal about them. Tell your most optimistic friends about them. Take risks with them.

3. Once you know what kind of environments are life giving to you, spend more of your time there. Once you know what kind of environments make you feel like you've never reinvented at all, spend less time there. Be honest with yourself. Invest in places where you are treated like a butterfly.

GETTING UNSTUCK

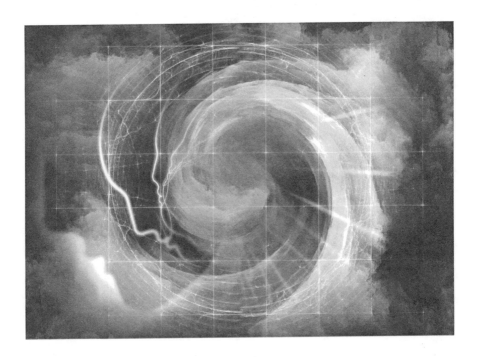

INTRODUCTION

Reinvention is a journey. Like any journey it is likely that something will happen along the way that will temporarily delay progress. The car breaks down, the traffic backs up, or we take an exit ramp from the process. However we may think of it, we get stuck. Our forward progress stops until we get unstuck.

Since reinvention is a highly personal process, different things cause each of us to get stuck. Some of the chapters in Part Two may not apply to you at all. Skip them. Other chapters may address an issue where you get stuck every day, so you may need to read them frequently to stay unstuck.

Some reinventors are helped by scriptural references. In the chapter "Dealing with Your Inner Critic," we take you through the three temptations of Jesus as a way of talking about the inner obstacles to reinvention.

One of the major sticking points for reinventors is discerning how to avoid getting tripped up by the failed expectations of family, friends, and communities. The chapter "Dealing with Letting Go" offers a unique perspective on this challenge.

As necessary as letting go may be, it does not come without a sense of loss. "Dealing with Grief" provides important insights on how to avoid getting stuck in grief by over remembering or under remembering the past.

There is a chapter on "Dealing with Suicidal Thinking," which is not meant to replace a deeper treatment by a professional and is obviously not for everyone.

But we find that suicidal thinking is much more common to the reinvention process than people may realize and, when unaddressed, becomes a place where people get stuck.

Since different parts of the reinvention process can be exhausting we wrote quite a bit in the chapter "Dealing with Fatigue." Reinvention is a marathon. Finding the energy to keep moving forward is a critical issue.

The final chapter, "Dealing with Now," is different from all the others in Part Two since it doesn't address a particular area where folks get stuck as much as offer a picture of what can happen if you don't get unstuck. There are few stories more painful to hear than those told by persons at the end of their lives when it is too late to reinvent.

6

DEALING WITH
YOUR INNER CRITIC

There is no better example of internal obstacles to reinvention than the temptation of Jesus. Apart from the account of his trial and crucifixion, the most detailed account of any experience in the life of Jesus is the description of the time between his first life and his reinvented one—the wilderness temptation. This occurs during the commitment phase of his reinvention.

The process of reinvention is often isolating, sometimes laced with anxiety about material security, and generally calls for some of the toughest work one will ever do in resisting the internal voices that lead to abandonment of the process. For Jesus, these temptations were powerful, soul-shaking, brass-knuckled encounters. The same may be true for the reinventor following this path. We believe there is much to learn about the inner struggles of commitment from this account of Jesus' temptations. Following are the three specific temptations from Matthew 4 (NRSV).

"If you are the Son of God, command these stones to become loaves of bread." (v. 3)

This temptation represents considerations of material security and the power of those to thwart one's process. Many people abandon a process of reinvention because it creates too much financial uncertainty. While stewardship of one's resources and responsibility for others are worthy considerations, it is important to keep these in perspective. Many people in the United States can live abundantly with less than they have, in some cases much less. Since a large amount of our anxiety is based upon comparative dissatisfaction, we offer a global perspective.

If you have an annual income of $20,000 in the United States, you are in the top 11 percent of the richest people in the world. As another therapeutic adage would say, "Comparison is the thief of joy." For many the cage door is open; they simply won't make the material adjustments that reinvention might require. The temptation to value those things above one's spiritual, emotional, and physical health, or even one's safety is powerful. Many people succumb to it. It is easy to do.

"If you are the Son of God, throw yourself down." (v. 6)

This is the temptation to control how others think of you, either by suicide or drama. As you have already seen, Jesus's reinvention cost him a number of relationships and public disapproval to boot. We all need relationships. But before you abandon your process of reinvention for the sake of the opinions of others, there are a number of things to consider. While there are often relationship losses during reinvention there is a corresponding gain in clarity about the nature of the relationships that remain. It is a process of distillation. As a public figure, Fe long wondered why people were in relationship with him. Reinvention gave the answers, sometimes painful, sometimes reassuring, and sometimes surprising. As a person who had worked for twenty years in opposition to gay ordination, imagine the surprise when one of the persons that reached out to him in a critical moment was a gay man. It was ironic indeed.

As you go through a process of reinvention, others begin to "fit" your life in a way that they could not before. For example, when Jesus lost the esteem of his family, he refused to withdraw into self-pity or capitulate to their opinion of him. When his mother came to the home where he was teaching with the intention of "taking him away," he looked at the people about him and said, "This is my new family."

"'All these I will give you, if you will fall down and worship me." (v. 9)

Nothing can more effectively derail an ambitious career track than a reinvented life. And nothing can more effectively derail the commitment stage of reinvention than ego and ambition. Reinvention creativity requires that one goes back to feeling inadequate, insecure, and underequipped to do new things. Even the CEO of a Fortune 500 company will look and feel like a toddler if he or she is learning to play a new instrument. In Gallup's 2013 State of the American Workplace study, 70 percent of those who participated described themselves as "disengaged" from their work.[1] One might wonder why so many people choose to stay in positions that they don't find engaging. Some of them are likely staying because of the benefit to their ego or their professional status.

Each one of these three temptations to abort reinvention is powerful enough on its own, but they tend to reinforce one another. Concern about the opinions of others leads to striving after power. Anxiety over material security leads one to cling to positions of power, which leads to a risk-averse investment in the status quo.

Your inner critic will remind you of each of these things as often as you allow it to. But remember these words of Teddy Roosevelt from a speech he delivered at the Sorbonne in Paris in 1910: "It is not the critic who counts; not the man who points out how the strong man stumbles, or where the doer of deeds could have done them better. The credit belongs to the man who is actually in the arena, whose face is marred by dust and sweat and blood . . ."[2]

As with any temptation, forewarned is forearmed.

DEALING WITH LETTING GO

In thinking about letting go, it may be helpful to observe that there are two movements in the life of Jesus that run in directions opposite to one another.

The first is restoration. Restoration is the drive to return something to its previous condition. The classic restorative process for relationships is outlined by Jesus: "If your brother sins against you go and tell him his fault, between you and him alone. If he listens to you, you have gained your brother" (Matt. 18:15, ESV). Jesus told a number of parables focused upon a restoration theme. The best known is the story of the prodigal son who is restored to a relationship with his father, but there are others. In the parable of the lost sheep, a shepherd searches for, locates, and restores an errant sheep to the flock. In the parable of the lost coin, a woman sweeps her entire home to recover a coin she had misplaced.

Children first hear these stories in Sunday school. Their retelling, enactment, and prominence shape the Christian consciousness almost to the exclusion of any other possibilities. As a result most Christians reflexively experience the spiritual obligation to try to restore what has become broken, damaged, or alienated back to its previous condition.

It is worth noting, however, that while Jesus taught these things, he never exhibited any restorative behavior in his personal relationships during his earthly existence. Pause for a moment and then think about it in a different way. Though Jesus experienced significant conflicts with his family, community, religious and political figures, and even his own disciples, there is no record of him ever approaching another person or group with the goal of mending or working on a relationship. The one exception to this observation is the restoration of Peter to his position of leadership after the denial of Good Friday. (But this happens after the resurrection.)

Some may find this shocking to hear, largely because no one has ever said it to them before. Some may even feel resistant to it at first. We simply invite you to let the truth of it sink in as we reiterate the point. Jesus *did* teach about restoration. We make no argument to the contrary. But there is no record in scripture that he practiced it himself. While one could engage in theological banter about the significance of this distinction, we would like to make one point that feels obvious, regardless of your theology. While Jesus' primary pattern of behavior was inarguably relinquishment instead of restoration, it is given virtually no attention in Christian teaching and preaching.

Relinquishment, the second movement in the life of Jesus, is letting go to move forward. In contrast to restoration, relinquishment is a major theme in both the behavior and teaching of Jesus. Jesus must repeatedly choose to relinquish elements of his past in order to move forward. This was an important element in the way Jesus dealt with his nuclear family. The evidence is clear. Jesus' family thought him to be misguided at best, demon possessed at worst. If he had chosen a course of restoration, he would have engaged in a process aimed at returning to the previous state of being the "golden boy" with angelic affirmations, wide-eyed shepherds, and gift-giving Magi. In a "family first" environment, Jesus would have given up on his reinvention commitment in order to restore family relationships.

Ryan was in the commitment phase of reinvention and kept getting stuck. As an aspiring artist, he found great creativity, risk, and energy in painting. But week after week, he would show his art to his spouse who responded less than enthusiastically, puncturing his creativity balloon. Ryan would leave Michelle's office full of optimism and hope only to return the following week again feeling suicidal and despairing. Finally the cycle was broken when he realized that his spouse might never embrace his art, but he needed to paint anyway. He followed the model of Jesus by maintaining his reinvention commitment and relinquishing a need for approval that was toxic to his very life.

We see one of the surprising aspects of the gospel accounts in the reference to women as disciples. "The twelve were with Him, and *also* some women who had been healed of evil spirits and sicknesses: Mary who was called Magdalene, from whom seven demons had gone out, and Joanna the wife of Chuza, Herod's steward, and Susanna, and many others who were contributing to their support out of their private means" (Luke 8:1–3, NASB). Many commentators have focused on the significance of their presence with Jesus. Few reflect on the significance of the fact that at least some of these women were married (as were some of the male disciples) and the implications of their itinerate lifestyle for their family relationships.

Jesus reserved some of his strongest exhortations for relinquishment in family relationships. When a man asked to go bury his father prior to becoming a disciple, a potentially restorative act, Jesus challenged him to "let the dead bury their own dead" (Luke 9:60 NRSV). He had a similar response to a vocationally stuck person: "No one who puts his hand to the plow and looks back is fit for the kingdom of God" (Luke 9:62 NRSV).

None of this makes for a counsel of disregard for one's family. Jesus taught that children should be responsible for the welfare of parents, which he demonstrated from the cross by placing his mother in the care of John, his "beloved" disciple. His prohibition of divorce is also placed in the context of economic justice and the need for divorced women to be protected from destitution. But it is also clear that the need for individuals to find a pathway to abundant living that expands the capacity for their purpose in the world may trump some aspects of family loyalty.

Reinvention may result in family disappointment or even alienation and still be a legitimate spiritual path. This is easier to accept when the family is clearly toxic: physically or emotionally abusive, addictive, or morally/ethically/legally corrupted. It is more difficult in cases where families simply want to maintain elements of the past that have been core to their experience even when maintaining the past is destructive to the reinventor.

Susan desperately wanted her husband to stop drinking because it was ruining their family life. Much to her delight, after fifteen years of marriage, he did. But she quickly found that he no longer could attend the parties they used to go to as a family. They started losing friends. She realized that she really missed the "fun" husband that he was when he was in an early stage of intoxication. Susan had to admit to herself that she wanted him to stop drinking, but she really wanted everything else to stay the same. In the face of a significant change in the life of a family member (even an "improvement"), most families would share that feeling, even if they would never admit it. They might have wanted you to "stop being depressed" and to "start being fun," but they may not be prepared for the ways that would require the entire system in which they exist to change. Here's the truth: when one person in a system changes, it requires the entire system to change. And systems hate change. This produces system anxiety that will often put pressure on the reinventing person to "go back to normal."

As with his family, Jesus' relationship to his community required an element of relinquishment. When he returned to his hometown, folks could not deal with his reinvention. They kept framing their relationship with him through the lens of his past: child, family connections, occupation. Jesus found his exchanges with people to be emotionally and spiritually draining. Mark 6:5 (NIV) says, "He could not do any miracles there, except lay his hands on a few sick people and heal them." So he left. He let go to move forward.

Both of us have struggled in different but similar ways with friends we had prior to our reinvention. We find it extremely draining to attend events or maintain relationships with those who are not prepared to be in relationship with our reinvented self. Many of these people are only interested in reminiscing about the past instead of finding out who we are now. While their intention may be generous and loving, those who are only willing to relate to us as we were prior to our reinvention can create a sense of loneliness and second-guessing.

Some might argue about the futility of a "geographic fix." If people can't run away from their problems, some might argue that they might as well stay put and deal with them. Some problems people will take with them wherever they go. That is true. Sometimes. Here is the rest of the story. Many reinvented people will find themselves thwarted and exhausted if they stay in their "first" communities and try to recover those relationships under a new identity. Jesus could have stayed in his hometown and tried to work things out. Instead he let go to move forward. He relinquished.

Let's just say it: some things can't be fixed. Some people will never respond to whom reinventors have become. Trying to eke out a different response is a waste of time and energy. We didn't say that. Jesus did. "If anyone will not welcome you or listen to your words, leave that home or town and shake the dust off your feet" (Matt. 10:14, NIV).

Fe once heard a sermon where the preacher said, "We should add another sacrament in the church. It should be the Sacrament of Kicking Dust." We have come to agree with that.

"The Missing Sacrament"

Shake the dust off your feet.
Do not carry the shame of failure
into the next town of your work,
lest a former work contaminate a new one.
Shame of failure can slay a soul.

Don't ask forgiveness for your shame!
It cannot be forgiven away or repented away.
Like a venomous viper
it can only be shaken off,
between conversations, or moments of giving,
or from one day to the next.

Shaking off the dust of shame
is permission to quit the past,
to say enough is enough,
to quit outwardly but inwardly as well,
to let the mind stop its processing
of what could have been
in preference for yet can be.[1]

8

DEALING WITH GRIEF

**"By the rivers of Babylon we sat and wept
when we remembered Zion."** (Ps. 137:1, NIV)

(Michelle's voice)

These words from the psalmist are dear to my heart. Partly because they were so beautifully put to music by Don McLean in the 1970s and then poignantly used in a memorable way by the creators of *Mad Men*. But they are resonant of the realities of my own reinvention experience to the extent that sometimes still, I need to sit down and weep for my life that is no longer. The home I once knew that no longer exists outside of my memory. There are things that have been lost through my reinvention that cannot be reclaimed. I wouldn't trade this new life for any of it. But it's also true that there is an element of sadness that is a quiet but steady companion with me on this journey.

As I reflect on some of the places people get stuck in reinvention, the tightrope of grief seems to be one of them. To fall off on one side results in sustained, prolonged, unresolved, or complicated grief that impedes one's ability to move forward. To fall off the other side results in unacknowledged and unaddressed losses from which one is never extricated.

No one needs to tell a person in reinvention that there will be losses or what they will be. For one thing, losses aren't the same for everyone. The likelihood that one can get through reinvention without substantive losses seems virtually impossible. The changes that accompany reinvention don't just impact one aspect of life; they often sweep through everything from one's faith to one's relationships to one's vocation to the way one dresses. The result is a variety of losses that can include the loss of relationships, home, identity, reputation, trust, security, faith, and financial freedom. I would argue and hope that every one of those losses will ultimately result in a subsequent gain that overshadows the loss, but the loss remains.

How one navigates those losses is pivotal to emotional health for the reinvented. Here are some ways one can fall off on one side or the other of the tightrope of grief.

The Trap of Bottomless Grief

Bottomless grief that keeps a reinventor stuck can take a variety of forms. Here are a few of the major ones.

Nostalgia and amnesia. In a speech to a crowd at Baylor University, biblical historian Walter Brueggeman cautioned the audience to avoid the twin temptations of amnesia and nostalgia in relating to the past. *Amnesia* is not remembering enough. *Nostalgia* is remembering too much. Both can be traps for missing the new thing God is trying to do in one's life. While the losses of reinvention are real, it is also true that grief can make one rewrite history in unhelpful ways.[1]

The extent to which people idealize past relationships or contexts is the extent to which they will be tempted to want to return to them. Every Christmas I get romantic ideals about warm, glowing lights of Christmas trees, special family recipes, and meaningful conversations where I am known and loved.

Every Christmas, I find myself more disappointed than joyful when I actually show up at parties to find that there's nowhere to sit, it's too noisy to talk, and few people there care to hear what's really going on at my deepest levels. The nostalgia for Christmases past is an idealized one that likely never existed in the first place. Or perhaps is a compilation of every positive memory from Christmases past, one happy snapshot at time, which creates a collage of what my mind's eye tells me life "should" be. It's not an accurate portrait of what has been left but instead the best parts of every portrait, all mixed together, which create a Picasso-esque dreamlike fantasy. Here's the problem: when that idealized picture is the comparison, one will struggle to ever be satisfied with the new picture, the real one. As I've said before, "Comparison is the thief of joy."

Brueggeman said in his address that "in exile, as illustrated by Psalm 137, the people of Israel longed for a return to a perfect Jerusalem that bore little resemblance to the imperfect city of economic injustice in which their ancestors lived. . . . They remembered a Jerusalem that didn't exist. They over remembered. . . . .Their displacement had given them a more perfect memory so that they screened out what was unseemly for the sake of certitude."

Likewise, Brueggeman argued, the twin to nostalgia is amnesia. One phenomenon that has been studied and proven is something called rosy retrospection. It is the tendency to both remember past events more positively than they were experienced at the time and to more quickly forget negative interactions. This common experience is called seeing the past through rose-colored glasses.[2]

This is not without its strengths but it can be detrimental to reinvention when people allow their imaginations to remember fondly a past that, in actuality, caused them a great deal of pain. Many abuse victims have returned to their abuser because, upon getting away from the person, forgot how torturous the situation was that they left in the first place.

Both amnesia and nostalgia can contribute to a prolonged grief that when unaddressed can compromise someone's ability to walk past the clarity doorpost that reads, "I let go."

Guilt. The most classic situation around which people grieve is related to death, where the possibility of return is not an option. While death is the ultimate loss, and in that way seems like the worst kind, it can be simpler than grieving reinvention losses. In reinvention people are often grieving elusive and nebulous losses that while more theoretical than actual may be no less painful. They are often grieving the loss of what never was that they now realize will never be. They are grieving that some relationships may never be healthy, likely never were, and need to be corralled with limits for the sake of their zestful, purposeful living. They are often grieving the lives they will never get to live and the people they love who will never become the people they had hoped. They are grieving the selves they will never actualize and the pain they have caused those for whom they care. These griefs run deep and wide. The pain of working through these losses is often intensified by the knowledge that reinventors might be able to return and make it right if they could just ignore that pesky doorpost that says "I matter, too."

What Grief?

While over-extending grief can be a trap that risks one's ability to move forward, so is the denial of appropriate grieving. Grief is a highly normal process of emotional suffering that happens to someone who has experienced loss. It is characterized by a powerful pining for the lost, great difficulty moving on, poor concentration, and a sense that life is meaningless. Even normal grief is intense and can temporarily sap most of the energy required for us to navigate daily life. But a normal grief process is a trajectory with movement, markers of improvement, and an ultimate end point.

Research shows that not everyone grieves the same, and some show little symptomology related to grieving after a loss. This is not a sign that those people are unhealthy or maladjusted. It is not appropriate to insist that everyone take the time to grieve. It is important, however, to recognize that it can be maladaptive when one is intentionally not grieving significant losses. As Brene Brown said in her TED talk, "You cannot selectively numb emotion. You can't say, 'here's the bad stuff, here's vulnerability, here's grief, here's fear, here's disappointment, I don't want to feel these. . . . ' When we numb those, we numb joy, we numb gratitude, we numb happiness."[3] Attempting not to feel the pain of loss will ultimately sabotage our reinvention and robs us of zestful living.

The goal of grief work is not the elimination of pain. It is freedom from being driven by pain. Certain tragic deaths, traumas, and irrecoverable losses will stay with people forever. That is not the same as grief. Grief is an acute state that is time limited and journeyed through. The pain of loss is a continuous state that cannot and should not hold up our reinvention. A healthy orientation to loss is to live redemptively into it as the flip side of love. Love inevitably involves the pain of loss; the two are inextricably bound together. An effort to remove all pain from love removes all love from life.

9

DEALING WITH
SUICIDAL THINKING

Suicidal thinking is a common experience for those going through a reinvention process, especially during the collapse phase. If you find yourself thinking about suicide as an option, and you've identified that it's primarily a symptom that your life needs to change, you have two tasks. You have to 1) find ways to stay safe, and 2) reinvent yourself as a pathway to changing your suicidal thinking.

Both are important. Changing suicidal thinking is a long-term process. On the one hand, it is important to have a plan to stay safe as you are doing that reinvention work. On the other hand, simply keeping you safe day-to-day is not an adequate solution without some longer-term approach that removes suicide as a viable option from your thinking.

Staying Safe for Now

In Applied Suicide Intervention Skills Training (ASIST), the helper is taught to listen deeply to how suicide became an option. Oftentimes those who do not experience suicidal desperation understand these ideations to be "crazy," "irrational," or "selfish." Not only is that kind of thinking unhelpful to the person considering suicide, but it also is dismissive of what, from his or her perspective, is a perfectly logical way to solve the problems. While suicide is never the best answer, it certainly has a rationality about it to the person experiencing desperation to the point of longing for death.

It is important for those who are considering suicide to know that there are three thinking errors common to almost all those in that painful state.

One. As true as it may seem, the assumption that it will always feel this way (or worse) is probably false. In a study of persons who survived a suicide attempt off the Golden Gate Bridge, 90 percent of them died natural deaths. Put another way, the overwhelming majority of people who attempt suicide while thinking life can never get better, find that life does get better, better enough that they ultimately do not kill themselves.

This is reinforced by the fact that the suicide rate for women is less than that of men, even though women attempt suicide at a rate five times higher. The reason appears to be that they use ingestion as their means much more frequently than men. Since ingestion is often reversible (as opposed to a gunshot wound to the head), women tend to live through the moment of crisis and discover that life does indeed get better.

Whatever your concept of an afterlife, we venture to say that the discovery of unlived and now unlivable experiences is a regret that never goes away. Sidney Smith, a nineteenth-century Anglican cleric wrote, "Regret for the things we did can be tempered by time; it is regret for the things we did not do that is inconsolable." A premature death by our own hand wiping out years of possibility would fall into the inconsolable category. This is captured well in Fe's poem "A Second Day."

> I am the faint light of the street lamp
> poking through your bedroom blinds
> to fall across your face
> when the drowsiness of death
> pulled down on your eyelids.
>
> I am the surprise party you almost missed
> the one when you caught her

looking at you in wonder,
The phone call you took on the last ring
from someone just thinking of you.

I am the heart you almost shattered
and the laughter you almost silenced,
a hundred close calls in a row . . . [1]

In the biblical account of the betrayal of Jesus, the action of Judas was hardly worse than the denial of Peter. However, Peter stuck around long enough to be forgiven (and reinvented!) while Judas did not.

Two. The assumption that asking for help makes a person weak or pathetic is not true either. No one accomplishes anything significant apart from the help of others. Asking for help is actually a mark of wisdom and maturity.

A little boy was spending his Saturday morning playing in his sandbox. He had with him his box of cars and trucks, his plastic pail, and a shiny, red plastic shovel. In the process of creating roads and tunnels in the soft sand, he discovered a large rock in the middle of the sandbox.

The boy dug around the rock, managing to dislodge it from the dirt. With a little bit of struggle, he pushed and nudged the large rock across the sandbox by using his feet. When the boy got the rock to the edge of the sandbox, he found that he couldn't roll it up and over the wall of the sandbox. Determined, the little boy shoved, pushed, and pried, but every time he thought he had made some progress, the rock tipped and then fell back into the sandbox.

In one final effort, the little boy grunted, struggled, pushed, and shoved, but his only reward was to have the rock roll back, smashing his chubby fingers. Finally he burst into tears of frustration. All this time the boy's father watched from his living room window as the drama unfolded. At the moment the tears fell, a large shadow fell across the boy and the sandbox.

It was the boy's father. Gently but firmly he said, "Son, why didn't you use all the strength that you had available?"

Defeated, the boy sobbed back, "But I did, Daddy, I did! I used all the strength that I had!"

"No, son," corrected the father kindly. "You didn't use all the strength you had. You didn't ask me." With that the father reached down, picked up the rock, and removed it from the sandbox.

Reinventing your life will require all the strength a person has and all the strength they have includes those who are able to help.

Many persons have never had to ask for help at such a deep level so they don't know how to do it. A little practice saying the words in private can help. First, say to yourself, out loud, "I need help." Hearing yourself say those words is an important initial step. Second, determine what you need help with and practice asking for that. You will need help from others during the reinvention process. This need will become particularly important if you are struggling with suicidal thinking.

Three. The assumption of being all alone is likely false as well. When living in a state in which a person so undervalues one's life that he or she deems it not worth living, it is nearly impossible not to project that attitude upon others. In addition the shame of suicidal thinking leads one to assume that the primary response of others will be one of shame as well. (This is a particular trap for perfectionists.) In fact the more common response of others is usually a fear of losing someone they care for.

Adding these three amendments to your mindset, what is your responsibility in keeping yourself alive?

- Find someone that you trust and tell them exactly the words you are saying to yourself, for example, "I am thinking my family would be better off without me." Thoughts that live only in your head have a power that is released once they are spoken.

- Don't stop at one person. Tell two or three. This community of support will build your connection to life. It will also be reassuring to each of them that they are not bearing this responsibility alone.

- Don't tell everyone and don't announce it on social media. Not everyone can handle it and telling too many people can have unintended negative consequences. It can result in people no longer taking you seriously, considering you something like the boy or girl who cried wolf.

- Not everyone will be able to help, but you will know after watching their reaction. Some people will be thrown into crisis by your admission, and you will end up taking care of them. If a person can't help you, find someone else.

- When you find yourself tempted to kill yourself, call one of the persons you have told. Don't assume that you only need to say it once. Suicidal thinking probably took time to take root and develop in your mind. It will take time for its hold on you to subside.

- Tell your community of support what you need from them. If you aren't looking for pity, tell them that. If you need someone to remind you to eat, to come sit and hold your hand, to not speak but to be present, or to distract you with what's going on in their lives, tell them that. People who want to help don't always know what to do but will be happy to help you if you tell them how.

- If you can't reach someone when you are in trouble or you do not feel safe after talking, call the National Suicide Hotline: 1-800-273-TALK (8255) or check yourself into the emergency department of a local hospital. Simply go to the registration desk and say, "I am thinking about killing myself. I need help staying alive."

Just for the record, none of this is theory. Fe has taken all these steps himself.

It is important to realize that not everyone is comfortable talking about suicide. It is impossible to speak in general categories about those who might be able to help. For example, we might encourage you to talk with friends, but some friends will be able to help you and others will not. Some family members will be able to help you; others will not. Some clergy will be able to help you; others will not. Some therapists will be able to help you; others will not. Recognizing this is important for keeping your expectations at an appropriate level. Some persons who are the closest to you may not be able to help you.

Of all the promises we make in this life and all the reinvention possibilities that we discuss in this book, none of them is possible if you don't stay alive. And we, for two, are happy you have. Make the call. Get the help. And then start reinventing your life.

Dealing with Suicidal Thoughts: Changing Your Thinking

(Fe's voice)

While staying safe in the short term can happen relatively quickly, changing suicidal thinking can take time. If you have determined that your thoughts of suicide are a signal that your life needs to be reinvented, you can expect that the cessation of suicidal thinking will take about as long as your reinvention process, usually several years. Think about suicide like you would a warning light on the dashboard of your car; it won't go off until the engine has received the attention it needs.

While this may sound discouraging I have found that suicidal thinking can play an important role in your reinvention process as long as you are willing to take the steps to stay safe. Trying to simply turn off suicidal thinking probably won't work for long because it is often there for a reason. Again, disconnecting the check engine light on your dashboard before attending to your engine is not a good idea.

I wrote about the role of suicidal thinking for transformation in *A Second Day*. (A Second Day person is one who has lived through a period of suicidal thinking.) Since I haven't found a better way of saying it, I will simply quote it here.

> In the movie *Adaptation*, John Laroche (Chris Cooper) is a brilliant but gritty character in passionate pursuit of rare, exotic orchids. Passion is the thread of his life's narrative. He engages an obsession to the point of mastery only to suddenly drop it and move on to the next. In contrast to Laroche, Susan Orlean (played by Meryl Streep) is a journalist willingly trapped in a successful though pedestrian life. She is beguiled by the throb of vitality in Laroche's life story. After she listens to him describe the car accident that killed his wife and knocked out his two front teeth, she responds by saying that she envies people who have had a brush with death. "It's like a free pass," she says dreamily. "It gives you an excuse to change your life in any way you want. No one would blame you."

> This then is one of the spiritual functions of suicidal thinking: it provides the owner of the thought permission for change that he or she cannot seem to find any other way. It is the kind of "free pass" that Susan Orlean longs for. Much like drug addiction, suicidal thinking is obviously not the preferred path of change. But some of us just can't get to the best side of life without it.

> When you realize that you are likely to kill yourself if you don't change your life (or at least live the rest of your life fighting that impulse), all reasons for inertia find their appropriate perspective.

Second Day people have learned to identify and weigh the proper alternatives. The choice is no longer staying with a toxic career versus leaving a toxic career. It is leaving a toxic career versus dying. It is making the break with a religious organization versus dying. It is deciding that you will stop trying to keep everyone happy versus dying. You see the pattern here. As Mark Twain put it, death "has a wonderful effect of clarifying the mind."

This is the potential gift that any pattern of self-destructive thinking brings to the soul. Once you gain this insight, you give yourself permission to make the changes that you would never allow yourself to make otherwise. For those of us who thrive on permission, the threat of suicide gives the soul an authority that we otherwise might never have allowed.

The threat of suicide gives Second Day persons permission to tend to their souls. Taking the time to connect to the deepest part of your being and the Universe of which you are a part are not luxuries. Neither are they duties imposed by the expectations of others. They are the air we breathe. When the demands of others press in on this time, we have permission to say "No" because we are ultimately dealing with life and death, not a simple time management issue.[2]

The threat of suicide gives Second Day persons permission to choose the people with whom they spend their time and to limit their contact with those who are toxic or indifferent. Some people are not safe for Second Day persons to be around. Unfortunately, this may, and often does, include family members. The soul of a Second Day person has the authority to decline invitations to family "celebrations" that leave them weakened, damaged, or at risk.

The threat of suicide also gives Second Day persons permission not to admit certain voices into their heads. Generally, I spend time weighing the merits of feedback given to me so that I can grow. But as one wise pastor once said, "not all voices are given equal weight in my life." Some voices, in fact, are arrows to the heart. They cannot be reasoned with or accommodated. Those voices must be denied admission. Second Day persons may have had trouble doing this in their

First Day since they might have felt guilty for refusing to listen. But when death is on the line, it is easier to place toxic voices on the other side of a soundproof shield and let them rant in silence. (First Day persons are those who, thankfully, have never seriously considered suicide.)

Second Day people often naively hope that this shift in perspective will be equally convincing to the First Day people in their lives. Given the choice "you can either have me (divorced, single, gay, religious, nonreligious, in AA, living with someone, fill-in-the-blank) or dead," First Day people often balk at the choice. That's because they tend to see suicidal thinking as an evil visitation upon an otherwise likeable soul. First Day people often want a kind of exorcism. They want you to keep everything in your life the same, with the suicidal thinking cleanly removed. They believe that suicidal thinking is some evil that has snuck into your otherwise wonderful life; in fact, it is a symptom that your life needs to change, often radically. When the tire drops off the edge of the highway onto a rumble strip, the noise is not a sign that your tires should be removed; it is a signal that you need to turn the steering wheel in a different direction.

For many persons, suicidal thinking becomes a way of coping; as the problems of life bear down and options for relief dwindle, the option of suicide offers a sense of control. As a reinventor begins to move out of the collapse stage and into clarity (I matter too/I let go/I am being transformed), better options begin to emerge that reduce the necessity of the suicidal option. Combined with work on the cognitive and spiritual dimensions of life, suicidal thinking finally loosens its grip after serving its purpose as a signal for reinvention.

10

DEALING WITH FATIGUE: ENERGY THROUGH HOPE

In science fiction thrillers where the seemingly impregnable and technologically marvelous space ship is engulfed by an unexpected crisis, the engineer shouts out, "Captain, we have lost power!" "No problem," the captain retorts, "Go to auxiliary power!"

What is the auxiliary power of the soul? When the sources of energy that typically fuel a person fail and the inner lights dim, where does one find the energy that reinvention requires? This is a critical question of the entire reinvention process. Collapse tends to deplete many of the sources of energy that have been dependable in the past: success in one's endeavors, the esteem of others, a financially sustaining job, a place to come home to, clarity of values, or a coherent philosophy of life.

These tend to evaporate at the very time that additional energy is being demanded by the creative process of reinventing one's next life. Where is that energy going to come from? As irritatingly simplistic as it sounds, that alternative fuel is hope.

In the triad of virtues listed in 1 Corinthians 13—faith, hope, and love—hope is the classic neglected middle child. If faith has to do with believing and even trusting what one *cannot* see, and love has to do with caring for what one *can* see, what is left for hope beyond some gussied up form of optimism? Is there any substance to hope that can arrest the inward "roll of the eyes" when it is offered as a resource?

Statue of the Tired Man in Mako, Hungary

One is tempted to think that hope is simply another expression of faith and love, or that if one has enough faith and love, hope will spontaneously happen. Any conversation with an experienced pastor, counselor, or thousands of bereaved families will convince you otherwise. Loving people of faith by the thousands take their own lives every year, and many others contemplate the deed, largely for a lack of hope. Faith and love alone are not sufficient to generate hope, any more than sticks and oxygen alone are sufficient to generate a fire. In 2010 the company BIC reported in an annual report that people spend more than four billion dollars on lighters, testimony to the fact that campfires don't light themselves.[1] A spark is required. Hope is the spiritual equivalent of a pocket lighter.

The power of hope upon a human being is hard to overstate. In 1955 a pioneering physician named Henry K. Beecher wrote a paper titled "The Powerful Placebo" that would change the course of medical research forever. Beecher had discovered that up to 35 percent of patients who received a pill would show significant improvement, even if it was a sugar pill, simply as the result of a surge in hope that they would get better. This meant that testing new medications would have to find a way of factoring out this power of hope, blandly referred to as the placebo effect.[2] Interestingly, the opposite is also true. The less well-known "nocebo effect" occurs when a patient experiences negative side effects on the warning label of a drug even when the "drug" is simply a sugar pill. Writing from his extensive experience of treating cancer (including more than one thousand melanoma cases) at Sydney Hospital, G. W. Milton warned of the impact of the delivery of a prognosis, and how many of his patients, upon receiving their prognosis, simply turned their face to the wall and died a premature death. "There is a small group of patients in whom the realization of impending death is a blow so terrible that they are quite unable to adjust to it, and they die rapidly before the malignancy seems to have developed enough to cause death."[3] Whatever reduces hope weakens us. As Proverbs 13:12 says, a loss of hope can make the heart sick or even kill us.

Hope is defined as a feeling of expectation and desire for a certain thing to happen. For a person in the process of reinvention, hope specifically is the expectation that a life can be fashioned that is more authentic, has a greater zest for living, is engaged with a community that is more resonant, and possesses a larger capacity to positively impact the world. Here is the rub: this hope must be nourished and sustained during a season of collapse when . . .

- Authenticity may be seen as a deficit in character rather than growth.
- The tasks of daily living are exhausting and leave little reserve for creativity.
- Family and friends are confused about what is happening to you and may even withdraw from the relationship.
- You wonder if you have anything to offer the world.

What Can Be Said about Hope?

Since hope can sometimes feel far away and abstract as a concept, here are a few practical thoughts on how to foster and cultivate hope.

One. Hope, like love, does not simply happen. In a John Mayer song, he reminds us that "love is a verb."

Now go back to that phrase from the song and substitute the word *hope* for "love," and you'll have the right starting point. Hope, like love, requires that you take action. If you wait to "feel" more hopeful, it is likely that you never will.

One of the tasks of reinvention may be engaging in the work of reinventing your relationship with hope itself and the ways you "strike the spark." If you have been accomplished in your previous life, you may have felt yourself in such control that you had little need for hope. Relying on hope may be a new experience for you.

Two. Hope is subject to what Stephen Covey calls "the law of the farm." He contrasts cramming for an exam with growing crops: "Can you imagine 'cramming' on the farm? Can you imagine forgetting to plant in the spring, flaking out all summer, and hitting it hard in the fall—ripping the soil up, throwing in the seeds, watering, cultivating—and expecting to get a bountiful harvest overnight?"[4]

You cannot "cram for hope." Hope grows organically, which means it must be seeded and nurtured over time. Expecting hope to suddenly appear if you have had little experience seeding and nurturing it will simply set you up for defeat.

Generating hope is often a matter of finding a different way of framing your situation. As one friend said, taking a step backward after taking a step forward is not a disaster; it's more like a cha-cha.

This is more than cute Pollyanna sunshine. We have found that such reframing of one's thinking, used with intentionality, actually begins to generate a more positive disposition toward the present and a more confident expectation for the future. The reframing that works for you, however, may be one you create given your own background and under the inspiration of the spirit.

An engineering professor once made the simple observation that a plane in total equilibrium cannot fly. The trick for a plane to fly is that it must be destabilized in a particular direction. During collapse it can be helpful to use that image by simply envisioning a plane and saying to yourself, "My life is not falling apart. It is destabilizing in a particular direction. I am flying." It makes a big difference whether you see yourself as falling apart or flying!

Three. In developing a positive expectation for the future, images are often more effective than words. A study looking at brain patterns in weightlifters found that the patterns activated when a weightlifter lifted hundreds of pounds were similarly activated when he only imagined lifting.[5] Mental imagery impacts many cognitive processes in the brain: motor control, attention, perception, planning, and memory. So the brain is getting trained for actual performance during visualization. It's been found that mental practices can enhance motivation, increase confidence and self-efficacy, improve motor performance, and prime your brain for success, all ways of nourishing hope.

Instead of focusing on problems, try visualizing what your reinvented life will look like.

Four. Exercise. The research is irrefutable. Regular, moderate exercise elevates mood and enhances a more positive expectation of the future. James Blumenthal, PhD, a clinical psychologist at Duke University, has explored the mood-exercise connection through a series of randomized, controlled trials. In one study, he and his colleagues assigned sedentary adults with major depressive disorder to one of four groups: supervised exercise, home-based exercise, antidepressant therapy, or a placebo pill. After four months of treatment, Blumenthal found that patients in the exercise and antidepressant groups had higher rates of remission than did the patients on the placebo. Exercise, he concluded was generally comparable to antidepressants for patients with major depressive disorder.[6]

Five. Get more sunshine. Higher serotonin levels in an individual generally mean elevated moods. Researchers found that regardless of the season, the turnover of serotonin in the brain was affected by the amount of sunshine on any given day. And the levels of serotonin were higher on bright days than on overcast or cloudy ones. The rate of serotonin production in the brain was directly relate to the duration of bright sunlight.[7]

But there is more. Increased exposure to sunlight not only makes you feel better, it may help you think better. Researchers from the University of Alabama found that among participants with depression, low exposure to sunlight was associated with significant levels of cognitive impairment.[8] Because collapse tends to contribute to a depressed mood at the very time that you need to be thinking more clearly and creatively, it just makes sense to take steps to get enough sunlight, natural or artificial, every day.

Six. Borrow hope from others. There are two ways you can do this. Get in touch with others who have reinvented their lives. Earlier in the book we referred to these as "othersiders." You can do this by reading their stories or viewing their video recordings. Better yet, talk to them on the phone. Or even better, sit down with them in person. This has the double benefit of inspiring you while also offering some practical suggestions for your own reinvention process.

This approach, however, doesn't work for everyone. People in the collapse phase of reinvention often feel that there are aspects of their situation that are unique to them or that other people have advantages that they don't have. The stories of others only make them feel more negative about their prospects.

The other way of borrowing hope from others is by spending time with those who see the positive possibilities, the "positivities" of your life. These may include a friend, a therapist, a spiritual director, or a family member. There are two key qualifications. First, they must know you well enough that their naming of the positivities of your life are realistic and credible. Second, they should not be so invested in your previous life that they get emotionally stuck when they think about you making significant life changes.

Seven. Develop flexibility in your thinking. Every strategy for nurturing hope requires an open mindset. Specifically, you must develop what we call a vulnerability for positive input. The human brain is hardwired for vulnerability to negative input that evolved eons ago in order to protect the species from life-or-death threats like saber-toothed tigers. When one is in collapse, he or she is likely to tune into this same brain circuitry that admits only bad news and argue with anyone who tries to tell you otherwise. This spiritual stubbornness is deadly.

You cannot control how you feel, but you do have control over your thought processes. When you receive positive input from people, you must take conscious steps to 1) admit it into your thinking, 2) reject thought patterns that negate that positive input, and 3) mentally practice a kernel of the positive input that trusted persons offer you.

Dietrich Bonhoeffer wrote in his book *Life Together* that the Christ in our own hearts is sometimes weaker than the Christ in the word of our brother or sister. Rejecting the hope that others offer us because we have so stiffened our minds through our own negative thinking is perhaps the greatest of all sins of the spirit. Simply responding with, "I receive that," can be the equivalent of opening our souls to the Christ who stands knocking on the door of our hearts.

Eight. Do something. Develop some realistic goals. Do something regularly—even if it seems like a small accomplishment—that enables you to move toward your reinvention goals. Instead of focusing on tasks that seem unachievable, ask yourself: "What's one thing I know I can accomplish today that helps me move in the direction I want to go?"

As we have said earlier, one obstacle to taking action is the paralyzing fear of making mistakes. Here it is important to reframe the meaning of a mistake. It is going to be difficult to develop a reinvented life with any breadth of understanding or depth of insight if you insist on perfection. Besides, who could stand to be around you?

It does not matter how proficient you were in your former life, you will be a novice in your reinvented one. An accomplished fifty-five-year-old trial attorney may be a master at winning personal injury cases, but if she or he decides that learning a new language is an important aspect of a reinvented life, she or he will feel like a baby learning to talk all over again. If you cannot tolerate being a novice, and the mistakes that go with it, better go back to your previous life.

The lessons you learn through your own mistakes are lessons that no one else can either own or take away. While acknowledging with Eleanor Roosevelt that we should "learn from the mistakes of others because we won't live long enough to make them all ourselves," a life built solely on hand-me-down lessons will always feel cheapened, usually at the end of life when there is no time left to do anything different.

Nine. Finally, tap into the spiritual resources of the *real* lives of your faith tradition, not of the idealized characters that have little to offer those treading barefoot on the gravel of real life. When Jesus went through his process of reinvention, his community accused him of putting on airs, and his family thought he had lost his mind. Buddha was married at sixteen but at twenty-nine left his wife and son to live an ascetic life. At one point his friends had to force feed him to save him from starving. In the difficult journey from a son living in Pharaoh's household to a liberator of the children of Israel, Moses killed a man. Abraham Lincoln became so depressed early in his career that his best friend had to remove his pocketknife from him. Connecting to such figures normalizes the struggles of the reinvention process and encourages an heroic response to those struggles rather than self-pity or resignation.

In a study of marathon runners, 43 percent of them indicate they "hit the wall," many of them at twenty miles into the race. One of the things they had started telling themselves was, "This is impossible." The solution? Many runners recruit a running partner who will do the fighting for them. Luis Manzo, PhD, a sports psychologist and running coach in New York City, suggests asking someone to jump in with you at a point in the run where you anticipate a struggle. "It can be a psychological booster shot when you need it," he says.[9] "If you're in the middle of a race with no buddy, Manzo recommends turning to the crowd for support. Interacting with people on the sidelines, even in subtle ways, releases endorphins. "One runner I worked with blew kisses as she ran by," Manzo says.

Reinvention is a marathon. Reaching out to others is critical in sustaining hope. Surprisingly, blowing kisses while you are on the race in whatever form that takes will actually help you finish the race. And who knows; someone on the sideline may need it too.

11

DEALING WITH NOW: AVOIDING REGRET

One of the burdens laid upon human beings is that of making choices. What many other animals do by necessity, humans must decide through what is often an anxiety-laden weighing of options. An unforeseeable array of future consequences adds yet another weight to schlepp down the road. Robert Frost captures this confounding limitation in the opening lines of his famous poem "The Road Not Taken":

> Two roads diverged in a yellow wood,
> And sorry I could not travel both
> And be one traveler, long I stood
> And looked down one as far as I could
> To where it bent in the undergrowth.

When it comes to reinvention, it would be kind if life allowed one to "be one traveler," to first travel down the road of reinvention to its outcome before making a final decision. The reality is that no matter how long one stands paralyzed at the fork and looks down either road, one can only see as far as it ends in the undergrowth of the unpredictable.

It is important for those standing at that fork to realize that the road more taken will be the non-reinventing road. This is not because it is a better road but simply because people have a tendency to take the road they know best even if another less certain road holds better promise. This is called the Ellsworth paradox. The basic idea is that given a choice of options, people "prefer the devil they know" rather than assuming a risk for a better outcome where odds are difficult or impossible to calculate. Put another way, people who are certain of being happy 5 percent of the time will tend to stay on their present course rather than take a risk for a life where there is a good chance, but no initial certainty, that they could be happy 95 percent of the time.

This outcome can be seen in the story of the rich young ruler. It goes something like this.

A young man who basically has everything discovers that he seems to be missing the most important thing: a life worth living. The urgency of his inner crisis is illustrated by the fact that he runs up to Jesus and falls on his knees. He asks, "Master, what must I do to find a life worth living?" The actual words are "what must I do to inherit eternal life" (Luke 18:18, NIV) but who would want to live forever a life that is not worth living? As one person put it, people are often concerned about living forever who don't know what to do on a rainy Sunday afternoon.

After reviewing everything that the young man had already tried—not committing murder, not committing adultery, not stealing, not giving false testimony, not defrauding, and honoring father and mother—Jesus now recommends a new path: find a mission and put your resources to its service.

Notice what happens next: "The man's face fell" and "he went away sad." The text says this was "because he had great wealth" (Mark 10:22, NIV). The additional problem was likely that the "way of riches" was the only road he had ever known—it was the road more traveled. Even though he was virtually certain that this road was spiritually empty, it was easier for him to choose the familiar road than a road he did not know, even though his chances of real happiness and fulfillment were better on the road of reinvention.

For humans, the tendency is to choose a path of certain unhappiness over a path that is less certain, but much more likely to be fulfilling.

While people can't "be one traveler" and travel down both roads to see where each leads, it is not the case that the roads end in completely unknown territory. In our experience there are a number of folks whose collapse was primarily driven by signals that life needed to change but who, out of fear, anxiety, guilt, shame, or apathy, take the non-reinventing road more traveled and come back with tales about what lies ahead on that road. Very often these are older adults whose souls have shriveled under the weight of their regrets.

As author Lewis Carroll of *Alice in Wonderland* fame is commonly credited with saying: "In the end we only regret the chances we didn't take." In her online posting with a similar title, Clare Hudson lists regrets of older adults before they die. The top five regrets of the road more traveled include:

1. I wish I'd cared less about what other people think. It's only when you realize how little other people are really thinking of you (in a negative sense) that you realize how much time you spent caring and wasting energy worrying about this.

2. I wish I had accomplished more. You don't have to have won an Oscar, built up a business or run a marathon, but having small personal accomplishments is important.

3. I wish I had told _____ how I truly felt. Even if the "one" doesn't exist, telling someone how you truly feel will always save you from that gut-wrenching "but what if" feeling that could linger for life if you stay quiet.

4. I wish I had stood up for myself more. Sometimes, it's too easy to think that if you go all out to please everyone you'll be liked more or your partner won't run off with anyone else.

5. I wish I had followed my passion in life. It's so easy to be seduced by a stable salary, a solid routine, and a comfortable life, but at what expense? [1]

Sometimes taking the road more traveled simply results in the gentle but sad realization of T. S. Eliot that the door people don't open might have led them to a rose garden. In other cases the impacts are more severe. Regret often shows up as guilt or bitterness.

Guilt. When people are not willing to admit that they need to let go because of what (or who) they can't change, the reinvention door disappears. In these cases, often a person's older years can turn into fruitless rumination and self-blame. When Michelle was a nursing home chaplain and would work with people suffering from early and mid-stage Alzheimer's disease, the ones who had missed the window for reinvention were often deeply stuck in a repetition of negative, self-focused ruminative thinking that is reflective of Erik Erikson's final developmental stage of despair. It is surely no coincidence that the highest suicide rates for any age group in the United States are for those more than eighty years of age.

Bitterness. Brenda and Harry were a couple who had been married for fifty-five years when they came for marriage counseling. Brenda, by both of their admissions, was deeply unhappy being a stay-at-home mom but never had the resources to launch out on her own and lived in a time and culture when women had fewer options. Brenda can identify when she wishes she would have reinvented her life—sometime in her forties. An astute (albeit undereducated) mathematician, she wanted to have a career where she was respected but took the road more traveled in her generation. Unable to admit to herself or others that she mattered too, she was never able to go through the door of reinvention. Now at seventy she blames Harry for all of her unhappiness. Harry can do little to make up for fifty-five years of pain and so he dutifully listens to her litany of disappointments (most of which are misdirected at him) week after week, which never seem to abate the bitterness she carries around.

The voices from the road more taken not only warn about these consequences of regret, but warn about health issues as well. Carsten Wrosch, a psychology professor at Concordia University in Montreal has been collecting life regret data since 2003. He has found that the emotional distress of regrets can trigger biological disregulation of the hormone and immune systems that makes people more vulnerable to develop clinical health problems, whether a cold or potentially longer-term health problems. But what's really surprising, Carsten says, is that most regrets were from decades past, often occurring when people were in their thirties and forties.[2]

In Michelle's work with clients, she finds that there seems to be a midlife "reinvention window" that opens to a person in their thirties, forties, and fifties. It has become fascinating to her in its predictability that virtually every person who calls for reinvention coaching is fifty-seven years old, as people around that age become desperate when they realize their reinvention window is closing. It's not exactly that the window snaps shut one day. But it is true that as a person ages and choices narrow, patterns solidify, resources constrict, and one's peak years slip away, a window that was hard to go through when it was open at its widest gets harder and harder to slip through as the opening narrows. And when a person misses that window they normalize reduced expectations for physical and emotional health, a significant purpose in the word, and an overall zest for living. Generally, the things that replace them are precisely the opposite of reinvention. Poor health. A lack of purpose in the world. A constriction of one's joy and vitality. It seems as a missed reinvention doesn't just leave a soul neutral and unimproved. The consequence of non-reinvention—when life's signals are calling a person to walk down the road less traveled—is erosion of the soul, which might be one of the most painful outcomes a life can take.

PART THREE

RESOURCES

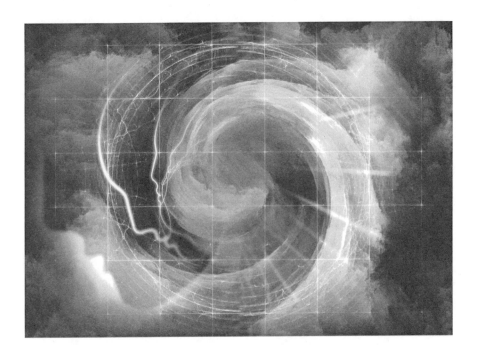

INTRODUCTION

For most people, reinvention is the most challenging season of life they will ever experience. The fact that we have written this book from both our personal and professional experiences with reinvention is testimony to our belief that the reinvention landscape cannot be traversed in isolation. This section is a modest beginning to a list of resources that you, the reinventor, might find valuable.

Without specifying a particular theological perspective, we believe that reinvention has a significant spiritual component that is essential. The chapter "A Reinvention Spirituality" offers some spiritual perspective and practices written from a Christian perspective that we have found helpful.

It is difficult for us to imagine navigating the reinvention process without the guidance of a professional. To that end, reinventors may find useful the chapter "Finding a Therapist and a Reinvention Coach."

Finally, and to the point that reinvention is not a journey that can be taken in isolation, we have included brief accounts of our reinvention stories. We have deliberately placed them near the back of the book rather than at the beginning to indicate that we are companions on the reinvention journey, not models.

12

A REINVENTION SPIRITUALITY

The person with the Spirit makes judgments about all things, but such a person is not subject to merely human judgments for, 'Who has known the mind of the Lord so as to instruct him?'" (1 Cor. 2:15–16, NIV).

The primary source of the grace, truth, and creativity required for reinvention lies within the human mind. The counsel of wise guides may be invaluable, but unless this serves to trigger a constructive internal response, all is lost the moment the reinventor walks out the door. The New Testament writer James speaks of this phenomenon as looking in the mirror and forgetting what you look like as soon as you turn away.

The Resource of the Mind of Christ

In the words of Christian scripture, this internal resource is known as the mind of Christ. The good news is that this mind of Christ is accessible to all who seek it and thereby acknowledge its existence. Because it is offered as a gift without exception this also means there are no excuses for living without its extraordinary capacities.

The mind of Christ is the source of all creativity exhibited in the universe. From the vast spiral arms of the Milky Way and the expanse of billions of galaxies like ours to the nearly limitless diversity of life upon the earth, all are expressions of the generativity of this source. The mind of Christ is the wellspring of all personal creativity as well. While the word *creativity* may trigger images of painters, poets, and performers, all human beings are creative. The most creative work you will ever produce will be the choices you make every day in connection with this source.

Volumes have been written on the spiritual journey and the disciplines that enable persons to access this reality. We will not attempt to summarize those here. A competent therapist will either be able to provide guidance in this area or make a referral to an experienced spiritual director. In this chapter, we will simply make an offering of the spiritual practices and perspectives that have been helpful in our reinvention processes.

The mind of Christ exists below the level of human thinking. Therefore it is accessed, not through our thoughts, but in the spaces between our thoughts. The purpose of many spiritual practices is simply to open up some dark space in the mind so that thoughts do not crowd out the flow of insight coming from God. It may be helpful to think of one's mind as a sky filled with the light of one's own thoughts. These thoughts are necessary to function in a world of time and space.

Now think of the stars as pinpoints of insight from the mind of Christ, offering the beauty of their light for your life. These are invisible from dawn to dusk because the daylight crowds out their light. When the sun goes down, space opens up for them to be seen. The darkness that creates space in one's mind is actually good. In the same way, one's myriad thoughts generally crowd out the mind of Christ. Using this image you can see how it would be possible for a very bright and beautiful person, even a religious one, to completely miss experiencing the mind of Christ.

In our experience, reinvention is nearly impossible apart from a living relationship with that spiritual reality. If people were able to successfully navigate the contradictions in their lives by piling up more thoughts in their heads, even good and profound ones, they would not have ended up where they are in the first place. A favorite saying from Alcoholics Anonymous is relevant: "Religion is for people who are afraid of hell. Spirituality is for people who have been there."[1]

Given this understanding of the mind of Christ, any process that simply adds more thoughts ends up obscuring the light one needs in the reinvention process. This can happen when one adds thoughts that are true and virtuous, even thoughts that are religious in nature, (and, yes, even the thoughts from this chapter!). Prayers that are simply comprised of a recitation of one's concerns can become an expanded mental zone of "concentrated worry" competing for the scarce space among the other thoughts in one's mind. Memorizing religious thoughts, precepts, or liturgies can be valuable in shaping one's thinking, but they can also trigger a cascade of other thoughts that lead to other thoughts, often accompanied by feelings of guilt or confusion. Our research with hundreds of churches reveals that many of our current spiritual practices and perspectives do not help the members of faith communities achieve their goals, develop healthy relationships, or feel positive about themselves.

Opening Space in Our Thinking

There is one experience that all human beings share through which they are all compelled to allow space in their thinking: sleep. Through the daily rhythm of sleep, spaces between thoughts open and creative impulses can break through. You may awake after a period of sleep with an unexpected insight or solution to a problem that you were unable to solve with your best thinking during the light of day. In a time when the culture was less hostile to a spiritual understanding of the universe, people have connected that experience to God: "I will bless the Lord who has counseled me; Indeed, my mind instructs me in the night" (Ps. 16:7, NASB). Even those of a more secular mindset still have these spiritual experiences except that they refer to what happens when "they sleep on it."

One way of thinking about spiritual practice is simply to replicate what happens in sleep during waking hours. When Jesus arose while it was still dark to go to a solitary place to pray, he was limiting the sights, sounds, and interactions that triggered a cascade of thoughts. By doing so, he was intentionally quieting his mind to allow inner spaces where the creative, healing power of God could shine through.

Plato tells a story that is useful in describing the state of our minds. He compares them to a ship where the sailors have mutinied and thrown the captain into the hold. Though they know nothing about navigation, the sailors take turns at the wheel, the ship going one direction, then another, with no ability to actually reach a destination. Little will change until the captain is returned to the wheel and the sailors take their rightful place under his command.

So we recommend several spiritual practices in order to help you take on the mind of Christ.

Thinking one thought. The first spiritual task of reinvention is to require that your thoughts take their rightful place in your mind so that there is space for the mind of Christ to emerge. Little else can be accomplished until you have initiated this process.

Try spending time each day in some exercise of thinking one thought to the exclusion of all others. The precise nature of that thought is less important than the exercise itself. The one thought can be counting breaths, tuning into a sensation in your body (like the rise and fall of your chest), repeating a word or sentence, or focusing on a scene in your imagination. By repeating this exercise on a daily basis, you are regaining control of the ship of your mind.

While it may feel like this exercise is making no contribution to your reinvention process, it is actually opening up space in your mind for the creativity of God to emerge. Research shows that folks who simply let their minds generate one incessant thought after another actually end up constrained by a lack of creativity. Paradoxically, they have greater cognitive rigidity than those who practice "one thought" exercises on a daily basis, and they also have a tendency to apply difficult or outdated solutions to easy problems based on their past experiences. The one quality you do not want in a reinvention process is applying outdated solutions that no longer work!

Capture learning. Once you begin to open your mind to the "stars" of creativity, you need some way of capturing what you are learning. This is the second spiritual task of reinvention. We recommend a regular process of journaling. You may see this as a contradiction. We have suggested exercises that restrict thoughts, but have also suggested a journal of lessons. How do you write down a non-thought? You cannot, of course. The mind of Christ will turn its guidance and insight over to your thinking process *after you have proven that you will not allow your thinking process to destroy it.* This is particularly important if you have a tendency to overthink or overanalyze.

One way of dealing with that tendency in yourself is to write in your journal in ink, preferably using a pen. Use ink rather than pencil because it is not easily erased. If you make a mistake in spelling, or think of a better way of saying something, don't cross it out. Place it in parenthesis instead. These simple insights can help counteract your own self-criticism, self-editing, and self-correcting—all forms of overthinking and overanalyzing.

Setting an intention. Finally, we recommend the spiritual practice of setting an intention, which is simply another way of deciding to take practical steps consistent with insight as it is discovered. The reinvention process runs on two rails. The first rail is restriction (of thoughts) and reflection (on insight). The second rail is action (practical, concrete steps) and experimentation (trying without self-punishment for failure). In the absence of either rail, the entire enterprise runs off the tracks. Without the first rail, you are likely to keep trying the same solutions that have stopped working or never worked in the first place. Without the second rail, reinvention becomes a fantasy that lives only in your mind or in the words of your journals.

Live in the moment.
You must be present to win.

In an age of social media, be cautious about prematurely publishing the insights that are emerging from the mind of Christ. Strange as it may sound, the divine mind is shy. Were it not so, God would be writing messages in the clouds. The hiddenness of God has its purpose: God can only be discovered through love. When you post the insights that are intended personally for you, it can shut down the creative process. By going public with your process too soon, the energy required to fuel your reinvention can become so diluted that words become a substitute for taking action. A skilled therapist can help keep your process running on both rails.

During a period of reinvention, the mind of Christ comes to your aid by supplying the creative impulse and orchestration of life events to move you forward in that endeavor. While others can offer support and practical guidance, they are unable to play a decisive role in your reinvention process. No one knows precisely how the mind of Christ is revealing itself within a particular person. As all good counselors will tell you, you are the expert on your own life.

While this frees you from being constrained by the judgments of others, it also makes you responsible for your own decisions. For persons who have been ruled by the opinions of others, this can be a terrifying step. You may be afraid of making mistakes. Undoubtedly you will make mistakes. But because they are your mistakes, you will also learn your own lessons rather than simply repeating the lessons of others. You will gain firsthand knowledge of how the universe works and move with the authority of that experience.

There are some things a person can only realize through that inner voice. When it is read in a book or spoken by another's voice, it sounds hyperbolic and unrealistic. But here it is.

The greatest obstacles to reinvention are in the human mind. However constrained you feel by external circumstances, the larger ones are inside. This does not mean that you cannot become anything you want simply by thinking about it. It does mean that there exists a reinvention specific to you and your particular circumstances that will expand your zest for living and your capacity to contribute to the world. The mind of Christ is working to bring reinvention to birth, but there are obstacles to be overcome.

Internal Obstacles to Reinvention

All obstacles fall under the two major headings of shame and fear.

It seems that it would be easier if reinvention were a linear, mechanical process that could begin on a drawing board in an engineer's office, move to the machine shop, then to the assembly line, and rolled out with a shiny coat of paint. For most people there is a collapse of one kind or another that is required to initiate the process. However severe that collapse, or whatever the cause, it is likely that they will experience some amount of shame.

Shame is the feeling of failing one's own standards or the standards of others. People experience shame even when they have done nothing wrong. They can experience shame over a number of things: Admitting you can't handle a career any longer, while others can. Admitting you have changed your view on something in a significant way, while your peer group has not. Admitting you are seriously considering suicide, when no one else you know is struggling with those thoughts. Whether you have done anything wrong or not, the shame can feel the same.

And shame can be a killer. In the movie *The Edge* a group of men are marooned by a plane crash in the Alaskan wilderness. Charles Morse is a well-read billionaire, played by Anthony Hopkins, who is trying to keep everyone alive.

> Charles Morse: You know, I once read an interesting book which
> said that, uh, most people lost in the wilds, they, they die of shame.
>
> Stephen: What?
>
> Charles Morse: Yeah, see, they die of shame. "What did I do wrong?
> How could I have gotten myself into this?" And so they sit there
> and they . . . die.

Shame fills up all the spaces of your mind and makes it difficult to connect to the mind of Christ. You may feel that you don't deserve to have God's help. You may feel that you are being punished. You may be filled with regret to the extent that you are so focused on the past that you cannot imagine a future. Shame can keep you so focused on failure, real or not, that you also fail to realize that collapse is a signal that reinvention is now the most important work of your life.

One of the remarkable, yet overlooked aspects of the ministry of Jesus is that he never interviewed people prior to helping them. He gave those who were lame, blind, and sick a fresh start on their lives, no questions asked. For all we know any of them could have been embezzling money, having an affair, drinking too much, or generally possessed of a foul mood. This quality of Jesus in his earthly life is one of the most important aspects of the mind of Christ. It is always working with you in support of new life. The mind of Christ is nonshaming.

All or Nothing Thinking

One of the enemies of reinvention after collapse is all or nothing thinking. Collapse does not mean that your life is a total failure or that you have failed everyone. Nor is collapse only negative. Collapse reestablishes your integrity by aligning the different aspects of your life. And it is painful when hidden aspects of your life become public.

A young pastor had resigned her position after several years of tough service combined with a disabling mental health condition that included suicidal thinking. During the resignation process, her personal problems became public. She was devastated. What was difficult for her to see at the moment was the potential of the new level of integrity that had been thrust upon her. Her inner life and her public life now matched. As people share about their reinventions, including some shame-inducing elements from their pasts, they often can say that the power of that transparency is life changing.

Be clear whether you are seeking reinvention or patching. Patching and reinvention occur on totally different time scales. You can patch up something broken in a few hours with tape and glue. Reinvention is a much deeper process that generally requires several years. For others to reestablish trust in who you are becoming does not happen instantly. If you do not align your expectations to the proper timeframe, you will become discouraged or abandon the process prematurely.

Reinvention is an organic process rather than a mechanical one. A mechanical process can be accelerated by applying more energy. If you push a car harder, it will go faster. An organic process is different. If you apply more energy to an organic process, you destroy it. Forcing a rosebud to open with your fingers does not produce a rose; it makes a mess.

Scripture refers to the organic nature of a spiritual process as "waiting upon the Lord." It does not mean that you sit passively. It means that you exercise patience for things to unfold in their own time.

Then there is fear. Fear is a particular challenge in a reinvention process. Fear is a double-headed viper. On the one hand, you fear the losses that reinvention will require of you. On the other hand, you fear the unknowns of a reinvented future. Taken together these fears can have three ways of scuttling your reinvention process.

1. They can damage the relationships you need to support you by making you angry and combative.

2. They can lead you to abandon the entire reinvention process altogether and seek refuge in some misshapen past.

3. They can paralyze you so that you move in neither direction.

There is enough knowledge about brain function to be able to pinpoint the area of the brain where fear is generated. It is in the "old brain" that includes the amygdala, hippocampus, and hypothalamus. The words *perceived* and *existential* are important. Existential means a threat to life itself such as one would experience from a wild, meat-eating animal or an armed attacker. The reality is that 99.9 percent of the time people are not dealing with either. Perceived means that one's old brain circuit cannot distinguish between a stressor such as missing a deadline for an important report and a saber-toothed tiger a few yards down the path. Unfortunately, the stress response is the same. People tend to respond in highly patterned, hardwired behavior that is not creative, that harms relationships, keeps people from achieving important goals, and generates a negative image of oneself.

Reinvention introduces stress into our lives. While the stressors are very rarely at the level of life and death, the brain reacts exactly the way it would if a car were to run over you. If you do not find a way to manage this reaction, reinvention becomes extremely difficult if not impossible.

One of the gifts offered to people through the mind of Christ is peace. Jesus said, "Peace I leave with you; my peace I give you. I do not give to you as the world gives. Do not let your hearts be troubled and do not be afraid" (John 14:27, NIV). These are not simply words of comfort offered in the face of inconsolable losses. Calmness of mind opens the door to the creative thinking that is essential for reinventing your lives. It enables you to set and achieve goals that are important to your success. It contributes to your capacity to form supportive relationships that are essential to your reinvention enterprise. It fosters a positive image of yourself so that you can begin to see yourself as a hero in your own reinvention narrative.

Thought Patterns That Generate Fear

In order to have the peace of Christ, we must bring our thoughts into alignment with the mind of Christ. This means identifying aspects of our own thinking process that generate fear instead of peace. Here are some examples.

Overgeneralization. When people have disappointing experiences with others, they may assume that is part of an endless pattern of negative behavior leading to extreme thinking, such as "No one can be trusted" or "Everyone is out for themselves." This attitude causes one to self-exile and abandon relationships that are important to one's well-being. Jesus did not generalize the behaviors of his critics to his disciples. Even as he was being betrayed by his critics, he never walked away from them and "having loved his own who were in the world, he loved them to the end" (John 13:1, NIV).

Disqualifying the positive. This is when people refuse to acknowledge the positive steps they have taken and become self-deprecating, "Anyone would have done that." They can't build a reservoir of positive self-regard that helps fuel their reinvention process because they keep polluting it negatively. Jesus was able to acknowledge the value of who he was, even in the face of Pilate and Herod, who considered him to be a fraud.

Shoulda, woulda, coulda. When things go wrong, people might think it is because there is something wrong with them. "I shoulda said it better." "I woulda succeeded if I had been smarter." "I coulda made it work if I had worked harder." Then they do not make it safe to experiment with different approaches because they punish themselves instead of learning from mistakes. Jesus did not assume there was something wrong with him when things didn't work out. He stayed focused on his mission.

It is important to deal with these kinds of thinking with spiritual brass knuckles. We will leave it to others to debate the personal existence of the devil. For some, it may be helpful to regard these anxiety-generating thoughts as lies of Satan. Jesus says that Satan is a murderer and a liar. In other words, Satan kills, not by possessing people and throwing them out of window, but by seducing them into believing lies. But whether this is helpful to you or not, it is true that if you do not recognize and renounce these things as lies, your reinvention is as good as dead.

Try this prayer of renunciation to accomplish this purpose.

> Lord I recognize that I have come to believe a lie, and the lie is . . .
>> that because one person has betrayed me, everyone will.
>> that when something I have done bears fruit, it doesn't count.
>> that when something I try doesn't work out, it is all my fault.
>
> I renounce this as a lie, and I replace it with the truth, and the truth is . . .
>> while some will betray me, many stand with me and always will.
>> while I make mistakes, I also am an instrument of God,
>>> and God uses me to bless.
>> that when something I try doesn't work out, there are things to be
>>> learned that will make other future efforts more fruitful. Amen.

Any step that can be taken to relax the mind is both consistent with the mind of Christ and critical to the reinvention process. There are a wide variety of approaches to relaxation and many have proven to have beneficial effects.

In their own way, each religious tradition maintains that a spiritual orientation to life is not simply the hood ornament of an otherwise secular existence but core to a life worth living.

Research bears this out. As stress accumulates over the years, brain scans reveal that the amygdala, the part of the brain that generates fear and all its cousins, tends to enlarge. Conversely, the hippocampus, the part of our brain that stores and retrieves short-term memories responds to accumulated stress by shrinking. In other words, as we age brains are hardwired to become increasingly anxious and unable to live in the moment.

Alternatively, we can exercise our prerogatives as spiritual creatures in ways that promote zest and newness of life. Adopting a reinvention spirituality is not only critical to the reinvention process but to the abundant living that Jesus promised.

A THERAPIST AND A REINVENTION COACH

As we have said throughout this book, we do not recommend that you try to reinvent your life without assistance. Supportive friends, family, and colleagues are irreplaceable, but a professional who knows the edges of reinvention and can help keep you from falling off is also an essential ingredient. Given the number of obstacles, amount of isolation, and potential risks of reinvention, we believe that having a responsible professional journeying with you will expedite your reinvention, raise the bottom on the low points, and be protective in relationship to the landmines. Here is a list of the primary tasks a professional can help you with in your reinvention.

1. Staying safe in the face of suicidal thinking.

2. Reframing your thinking in places where it is keeping you stuck.

3. Managing complicated relationships and toxic family system dynamics.

4. Processing negative emotions like grief, guilt, and shame in a healthy way.

5. Encouraging your creative energies as you try new things.

6. Cheerleading for you as you succeed at your own goals.

7. Asking good questions of your decision making to hold up a mirror for who you want to be.

While all of these dynamics are likely to be present in some form for the reinventor throughout the whole process, tasks 1–4, which would be best done with a therapist, are mostly going to be present in the earlier stages of reinvention. Tasks 5–7 are mostly going to be relevant in the later stages (commitment and coherence) and may be better accomplished with a coach.

While *therapist* is a profession that most people are familiar with, the concept of coaching is less so. *Coach* is a word that pops up more and more these days. There are executive leadership coaches, health coaches, and life coaches. The number of subspecialities in coaching is nearly dizzying and getting more so every day. But what all good coaches have in common is a methodology that doesn't immediately pathologize. While even the most strengths-based mental health therapists are trained to start with a medical diagnosis, coaches presume a starting point of health and see themselves as a journey-person for someone who has a goal and needs help reaching it. Much like the metaphor of a stage coach, it's not the coach's job to know the destination. It is the coach's job to help a person get there safely.

Of course the best person to help a reinventor would be a reinvention coach who is also a therapist. This person would be able to take these professional hats off and on throughout the course of your journey together in ways that fit best with where you are. When you need a therapist, this person could be a therapist. When you need a coach, he or she could just as easily be that. Unfortunately, if you were to Google the words *reinvention coach,* a search is going to yield very few, if any, results for such a person in your community. Very few professionals bill themselves as reinvention coaches, let alone therapists who do. It is our mission to work on changing that reality through the creation of a reinvention coaching program. It is our hope over the next few years to find pastors, clinicians, spiritual directors, and othersiders who are naturally astute listeners and train them in the ways of reinvention coaching.

But in the mean time, we believe that the best thing for you to do until such a cache of coaches exists, is to find a good therapist who you can feel good about working with throughout your reinvention. We would like to offer you a list of things to assess for finding a guide on your journey. Not all therapists can do reinvention work. But with the following guide in your hands and this book in theirs, we believe you can find someone who can helpfully assist you on your way.

When you're looking

- Ask other people. Look for someone who is skilled in helping others create a life that they can live with enthusiasm. The best recommendations are the ones that come from others this person has helped.

- Interview them and ask questions about their focus. Tell them you are looking for a therapist who can be a reinvention coach. Tell them that you don't think you are as broken as your life is and that you need help thinking about that at every level. Watch how they respond. If they look confused or seem skeptical, they might not be for you.

- Trust your gut. The best indicator of positive outcomes in clinical work is rapport. If you don't connect with him or her, this will not work.

- Watch how they model the way you wish everyone treated you in your reinvented life. They listen. They give you the benefit of the doubt. They see your strengths. They believe in you.

When you're meeting

- Their focus is not primarily on what's wrong with you, but on exploring what's right and true for you and with you.

- They are not afraid of your collapse. While they should be working to help you through that as quickly as possible for your sake, you should not get the sense from them that they are uncomfortable and therefore are trying to lift you out of collapse prematurely, "before the whole forest has burnt down."

- In the same vein, assuming you are not an immediate threat to yourself, they should be able to tolerate low-grade suicidality without being thrown into crisis or taking extreme measures. They will likely need astute suicide risk assessment skills.

- They are capable of unconventional thinking. While you struggle to think outside the box, whether it be vocational, relational, or theological, you should not find yourself constrained by their ability to do the same.

- They don't allow you to get bogged down by emotion. They don't allow you to spend an inordinate amount of time looking backwards. While able to explore those things to some degree, they are generally and primarily forward facing in their orientation.
- They ask you good and challenging questions like:
  > When was the last time you felt truly alive?
  > What would be your most ideal life if you could wave a magic wand and create it from scratch?
  > What are the questions you're afraid to ask?
  > What are the truths you're afraid to name?
  > What are the nonnegotiables that you don't feel able to change? Why is that? Allow your imagination to explore what would happen if they changed.
  > What are the "shoulds" that are keeping you stuck?
  > How does your thinking about your stuckness keep you stuck?
- They develop an action plan to establish a course of action for the future. It is important to realize that a reinvention process is primarily about action, not ideas or insight. Talk is not enough. Actions are also necessary.

Once in coherence

- Unlike some therapies that have clear points of termination, this person should be willing and able to check in with you as needed for the long term.

OUR STORIES

Michelle

I was raised by fundamentalist parents in a small town in the Appalachian country of western Pennsylvania. We attended two different churches growing up—one informed by a holiness tradition and the other informed by a Pentecostal one—but the religion of the place was nearly as culturally engrained as it was denominational. Into my adolescence, my parents fought an increasing amount, and it was more and more obvious to anyone who was paying attention that my mother was unhappy. Still, it never dawned on me that our beliefs were not all entirely right, that those who disagreed with our beliefs were not all entirely wrong, or that this good and insulated life we were living could ever be lost.

As a teenager in church, I was hearing one message while I was living another. Wild Saturday nights were followed by tearful Sunday morning repentance as a regular matter of course. I was dissonant in my beliefs and my behaviors, and it became clear that for some leadership of that church, the dissonance was the same as I experienced sexual inappropriateness from a trusted mentor. This was the second experience of that kind for me in a second faith community. Cracks were forming in my internal infrastructure.

Around that time, my youth group went to New York City on a weekend mission trip, and my way of life and all the above assumptions were seriously called into question. I did not have language for it at the time, but the exposure to all manner of ethnic, religious, and economic diversity in such a short time frame was a culture shock that altered the course of my life from that point forward. My small and narrow understanding of God ran into direct conflict with all the complexities of the larger world. New York's diversity of experience and sheer population size formed more and deeper cracks in my insular world.

I graduated high school nearly at the top of my class and went on to complete a degree in chemistry. That time in college was important as it was where I was introduced to thoughts other than those of my community at home. My mother "suddenly" announced she was leaving my father (which was a reflection of her own reinvention journey, where she was in collapse). My grandfather died in spite of all of our Pentecostal attempts to pray him back to health. The cracks were becoming crevasses, which in turn were eroding into canyons. And the voices of those disenfranchised in the Big Apple beckoned me to live out my faith in what seemed like the only consistent way I could think of. In a youthful desire to save the world, I returned to the urban mission in New York. Instead of going to medical school, as had been the plan, I packed up and moved to Queens where, try as I might, I could not squeeze that place or those people into my religious or cultural frameworks. I became best friends with a lesbian who was the most grace-filled person I had ever met. And no matter how many times I told mentally ill homeless men that "Jesus [was] the answer," they somehow still remained sick with nowhere to lay their heads. I was now in full-on contradiction. I tried to explore this contradiction with the religious community with whom I lived and worked, but all to no avail. In fact, my questions and doubts became so annoying to those in authority that I was asked to "stop spreading my poison."

In a last ditch effort to find a cohesive ideology that could make sense of the world but also retain my old biblical literalism, I moved into a conservative Anabaptist community in Brooklyn. I sewed up the slits in my skirts, put on a bonnet, and gave it my best shot. Once again—contradiction. Some people thrived in that place where roles were clear, expectations were explicit, and radical things were done in the name of the gospel. But there seemed to be a disproportionate amount of depression and sadness, especially among the women. I was becoming more emotionally fragile as well, and I felt the community gradually growing less able to handle the ambiguities that accompanied that fragility. In one conversation where a well-intentioned friend offered me his "ideals" about giving it all to God, I retorted, "If this thing of faith is about survival of the fittest, then I quit." And I did. I had collapsed.

I left my job as an eighth-grade public school teacher in the Red Hook neighborhood of Brooklyn and moved back in with my now divorced and remarried mother (who was moving into coherence in her own reinvented life). For lack of a better idea, and at the advice of a wise and dear friend (to whom this book is dedicated), I enrolled in seminary. My family either did not know what to do with me or felt angry/alienated by my choices. I cried every day for the whole first year of seminary as I heard things I had never heard before about social justice and feminist theology. I started seeing a therapist who really saw me. I sat in classes where professors were able to dialogue meaningfully about biblical truthfulness as it related to myth and poetry. I experimented with various theological and biblical paradigms, some of which I ultimately rejected and some of which I still hold today. And I started dating a fellow seminarian who was Presbyterian. Our marriage and my entry into the Presbyterian Church (USA), a tradition that puts great emphasis on the value of the mind, was the beginning of a new coherent and zestful life with increased capacity for contribution. This life is one that no eye could have seen nor ear could have heard nor could have been imagined in the heart of this naïve little Appalachian girl.

In my first life . . .	In my reinvented life . . .
Obese	80 pounds lighter
Smoker	Nonsmoker
Rigid belief structure	Flexible belief structure
Anti-gay	Gay friendly
Lived away from family of origin	Moved near family of origin
Angry	Grateful
Spent time working to "rescue" people	Spend time working to "know" people

Quick to cry	Slow to cry
Risk-taker	Cautious
Didn't go to church	Joined a church
Assemblies of God	PCUSA
Vocationally directionless	Have a career
Financially dependent	Self-supporting
Lived in one room	Own my home
Barely left the United States	Visited 18 countries on 5 continents
Listened to Christian music	Listen to NPR
Read the Village Voice	Read the Pittsburgh Post Gazette
Was a victim of clergy sexual misconduct	Work to end clergy sexual misconduct
Went to therapy	Am a therapist
Many friendships were mostly about the other person	Fewer friendship that are necessarily mutual
Ate meat multiple times each day	Vegan at home
Long hair that was dyed red	Short hair that is naturally gray
Didn't care about nature, the earth, or sustainability	Recycle, garden, and can
Binge drank alcohol secretly	Responsibly drink alcohol publically
Hated wearing shoes	Still hate wearing shoes

Fe

Igrew up in a conservative, Midwest home, raised by parents from a Free-will Baptist background who neither smoked and drank nor swore, at least in front of the children. I graduated from the Ohio State University with a degree in engineering physics after cramming a five-year program into a four-year period. During that time, I also became an evangelical Christian. I married in my senior year.

After three enjoyable years in research and development at the Eastman Kodak Company, I left to attend seminary, after which I was ordained as a Presbyterian minister. My communication and instinctive organizational skills combined with a genuine spiritual fervor made me an effective leader, and the churches I served grew in numbers, vitality, ministries, and facilities.

During those early years, I also became affiliated with a Christian community that practiced what I would describe as a strict, ultra-Calvinistic, and exclusive version of the Christian faith. I followed the community's teaching with vigor. I voluntarily restricted my reading to recommended texts, refused to enter into friendships outside of the community's circle, adopted a mono-cultural view of the world that was primarily white, upper middle class, and maintained a highly skeptical view of my own thinking and gifts.

In the mid-eighties I was called as senior pastor to a large, multistaff church for which I felt totally unprepared. Lacking any sense of confidence and sure of failure, suicide entered my list of options for the first time in my life.

I began reading again in the early nineties. One particular area of interest was the relationship between quantum physics and theology. The ability of quantum physics to live with paradox was a significant factor in developing a spiritual perspective during my college years. However any thought of integrating these two was discouraged at my conservative seminary, so I pushed that possibility aside. By 1995 I was teaching quantum physics to large classes in the church. Within three years, my theological perspective had radically changed, though I hid much of that from the congregation I served.

At the same time, I began to develop friendships with people outside of my faith community. I realized at that point that I knew almost nothing about what friendship meant. I had become so accustomed to vertical, authoritarian relationships that I had little understanding of what a mutual, committed, soul-sharing friendship might look like. I was forty-five-years old, but relationally I was a teenager, with all the intoxications and mistakes of a teenager.

Concurrently, I embarked on a spiritual journey that led me into healing contemplation. After a five-day, meditative, boot camp, the world looked totally different to me. I began to practice this healing approach on a limited basis with some significant success. It required about a half hour of time with a hospital patient and was quite different from the typical conversation and prayer that I had learned in clinical pastoral education. I felt torn: do I practice this more promising form of healing at the risk of developing a reputation as a "new-ager" or stay with more traditional approaches to pastoral ministry? Again, I hid most of that struggle from others.

The gap between who I was becoming and the person I was exhibiting became agonizing. As part of the expanding mission of the church, but also as an escape, I went to Honduras to explore mission opportunities. While the exposure to an entirely different culture was invigorating, it also challenged many of my political and ministry assumptions, deepening the internal divide. While developing a center for children with HIV, I also was trying to figure out how I could get myself killed, "suicide by mission."

In quick succession I precipitated a series of crises that lead me out of pastoral ministry, ended my marriage, left me tens of thousands of dollars in debt with no place to live, and landed me in the psychiatric room of the emergency department at the Ohio State University as a suicide risk. My wonderful therapist put it this way: "All your life, you have tried to avoid rejection and now the universe has given it to you in spades."

It is important that my therapist never placed me into a diagnostic category, but functioned primarily from an asset perspective. Viewing the near total rejection I was experiencing as a "gift of the universe" was strangely liberating. If "freedom's just another word for nothing left to lose," God was giving me a fresh opportunity to define my life, what I would later refer to as "reinvention." I had wanted to do organizational consulting for more than ten years but got pushback from the church I was serving. Now I could throw myself into that work with relish through a consulting company that a friend and I had started.

Creatively, my life exploded. I began developing assessment tools, designing and conducting training, authoring books, and doing public speaking. The work in Honduras engaged hundreds of people and raised hundreds of thousands of dollars to create a ten-building complex on top of a mountain now caring for three dozen children with HIV. I received suicide intervention training, assisted communities in developing suicide prevention plans, and trained thousands of people in suicide awareness.

I began to "own" my perspectives as valuable and my voice as a voice with something to say. As a single person, I began to date, which was to many, scandalous. For a while, many people saw me simply as a soul who had lost his way, and they kept trying to get back "the old Russ" that they had known and loved. The fact that much (not all) of the old Russ was a fiction was too much for most people to deal with. Many gave me up as a lost cause. A wonderful, priceless few made the journey with me, a gift that goes beyond words.

As part of my own drive to create coherence in my life, I changed my name to Fe Anam Avis. In addition, I developed a new symbol for my faith that brings together many of the core elements of my life. The "Magi" symbol can be found on the back cover of this book.

In my first life . . .	In my reinvented life . . .
I had a career and received a paycheck.	I have two businesses and live on what the businesses generate.
I was dependent upon an organization to decide what I should do.	I take the initiative to start things on my own.
I held conservative Christian beliefs.	I have adopted a process view toward Christianity.
I lived in a home I owned.	I lived in a room I rented.
I had many admirers.	I have a few very good friends and a number of detractors.
I wrote sermons.	I write books.
I was married.	I am divorced and remarried.
I thought sex was the greatest sin.	I think bigotry, hatred, and injustice are the greatest sins.
I prayed.	I meditate.
I ate beef.	I eat mostly vegetables and more healthy protein.

I relied on medicines to keep me healthy.	I rely more on lifestyle to keep me heathy.
I was Presbyterian.	I am Episcopalian.
I did a lot of teaching.	I do mostly training.
I thought nationally.	I think internationally.
I was a Republican.	I am a Democrat.
I bought jewelry made of symbols.	I create symbols.
I lived in one place and moved infrequently.	I live in many places and move frequently.
I worked in one place.	I travel in my work.
I used my birth name.	I changed my name.
I was most afraid of what other people thought of me.	I am most afraid of slipping back into suicidal thinking.
I sat all day.	I run three miles a day.
I put up with inappropriate behavior.	I choose not to be with people who are not good for me.
I waited on other people before I would have fun.	I go to movies and hike by myself.
I worked in an office.	I work in coffee shops and state parks.
I wore appropriate clothing.	I wear clothes that don't match.
I wore dress shoes most of the time.	I wear sandals most of the time.
I wore glasses for distance vision.	I don't need glasses for distance vision.
I mowed the lawn.	I grow flowers.
I weighed 200 lbs.	I weigh 165 lbs.
I took a daily anti-depressant.	I take a daily aspirin.
I regularly had an afternoon anxiety attack with GI distress.	I regularly take an afternoon walk to the grocery store and buy a glass of tea on the way home.
I was secretive about my suicidal past.	I tell people about my past.
I wanted to die.	I want to live and love as long as I can.

CONCLUSION

We believe that a significant percentage of persons, including participants in faith communities, are in need of reinvention. The problem is that these persons do not wear signs. The reinvention need presents itself under a number of guises: instances of depression, addiction as self-medication, increased suicide rates as women hit middle age and men retirement age, vocational burnout or dismissal, chronic illnesses, and poor-decision making.

Reinvention is a spiritual issue that touches deeply upon questions of meaning. Many persons feel they must leave their faith communities if they are going to seriously engage in a reinvention process. Oddly enough, if reinventors begin attending a different faith community only two blocks away, they will be welcomed with open arms. Many times, they simply leave faith communities altogether. As is true for othersiders in general, faith communities are often the first community they leave and the last community they return to.

The primary issue for faith communities is one of hospitality. There are undoubtedly tens of thousands of church signs indicating "Visitors Welcomed" or "Visitors Expected." Would the same hospitality be shown to reinventors among their own members? Is it conceivable that faith communities might one day provide Reinvention Teams to support folks on that journey? What kind of impact would it have on a faith community if it became known as a place where people could reinvent their lives? Our good friend Jim Hanna, a therapist and congregational consultant, says such a reinvention faith community would have to beat people away from the doors.

We intend to develop a number of resources over the next few years to support reinvention, including training for reinvention coaches and a manual for developing reinvention communities. We need the help of our readers to do so. After using this book, please go to www.soulshopmovement.org and give us feedback on how this book helped you or how we might improve future editions. Also let us know if you would like to be involved in the reinvention movement.

ENDNOTES

Introduction
1. Fe Anam Avis. *A Second Day* (MAGI Press, 2014), 16.

Chapter 2
1. Information from several sources and reports including: Associated Press: Aug. 2 and 3, 2007; Minnesota Department of Transportation reports: 2001, 2005, 2006; and *St. Paul Pioneer Press*, Aug. 23, 2007.

Chapter 3
1. Lawrence LeShan. *Cancer As a Turning Point, A Handbook for People with Cancer, Their Families, and Health Professionals* (New York: Plume, 1994), 225.

Chapter 4
1. Melinda Wenner, "Smile! It Could Make You Happier," *Scientific American* (September 1, 2009). www.scientificamerican.com

2. Goethe, "On Commitment," in *The Rag and Bone Shop of the Heart*, Robert Bly, James Hillman, and Michael Meade, (HarperCollins Publishers, 1992), 235.

Chapter 6
1. State of the American Workplace, Gallup. http://employeeengagement.com/wp-content/uploads/2013/06/Gallup-2013-State-of-the-American-Workplace-Report.pdf

2. Theodore Roosevelt. "Citizenship in a Republic," speech delivered at the Sorbonne, in Paris, France, April, 23, 1910.

Chapter 7
1. Fe Anam Avis. *A Second Day* (MAGI Press, 2014), 44.

Chapter 8
1. Ken Camp. "Resist the Seductive Lure of Nostalgia, Brueggeman Urges," *The Baptist Standard* (March 18, 2016). https://www.baptiststandard.com/news/texas/18916-resist-the-seductive-lure-of-nostalgia- brueggemann-urges#.VuxKkXbOxVA.facebook

2. Brian Neese. "Rosy Retrospection: A Look at the Psychological Phenomenon," Southeastern University online learning (February 23, 2016). http://online.seu.edu/rosy-retrospection-psychological-phenomenon/

3. Brené Brown. "The Power of Vulnerablity." TED Talk posted December 2010. https://www.ted.com/talks/brene_brown_on_vulnerability/transcript

Chapter 9

1. Fe Anam Avis. *A Second Day* (MAGI Press, 2014), 10.
2. Ibid, 89–91.

Chapter 10

1. Statistic Brain. http://www.statisticbrain.com/bic-company-statistics/

2. H. K. Beecher, "The Powerful Placebo," *Journal of the American Medical Association*, vol. 159, no. 17 (December 24, 1955).

3. G. W. Milton. "Self-Willed Death or the Bone-Pointing Syndrome," *The Lancet* (June 23, 1973), 1435–36.

4. Steven R. Covey, A. Roger Merrill and Rebecca R. Merrill. *First Things First* (Free Press, 2003) 55.

5. A. J. LeVan. "Seeing Is Believing: The Power of Visualization," *Psychology Today.* https://www.psychologytoday.com/blog/flourish/200912/seeing-is-believing-the-power-visualization

6. Kirsten Weir. "The Exercise Effect," American Psychological Association. http://www.apa.org/monitor/2011/12/exercise.aspx

7. "The Health Benefits of Sunlight." A Guide to Holistic Healing. http://www.natural-health-zone.com/sunlight-therapy.html

8. Effect of sunlight exposure on cognitive function among depressed and non-depressed participants: a REGARDS cross-sectional study. US National Library of Medicine, National Institute of Health. http://www.ncbi.nlm.nih.gov/pmc/articles/PMC2728098/

9. Nancy Averett. "Against the Wall," *Runner's World,* March 2, 2011. http://www.runnersworld.com/running-tips/how-to-avoid-hitting-the-wall-while-running

Chapter 11

1. Clare Hudson. "20 Things People Regret the Most Before They Die," Lifehack. http://www.lifehack.org/articles/communication/20-things-people-regret-the-most-before-they-die.html
2. Carsten Wrosch et al. "The Importance of Goal Disengagement in Adaptive Self-Regulation: When Giving Up Is Beneficial," *Self and Identity*, vol. 2, issue 1 (2003).

Chapter 12

1. Ernest Kurtz and Katherine Ketcham. *The Spirituality of Imperfection: Storytelling and the Search for Meaning* (Bantam, 2002), 15.